Pragmatic Talk

Everyday Conversations
실생활편

PREFACE

영어회화를 잘 하기 위해서
기억해야 하는 **가장 중요한 한 가지**는 바로

it's easy if you try.

'시도'하면 쉬워집니다. 가장 중요한 키워드입니다.

지금 책을 읽고 있는 여러분은 이미 시작이라는 첫 페이지를 넘기셨습니다.
여러분의 'try'에 박수를 보내며 지금부터 프레그마틱 토크가 최상의 결과를 위한
길잡이가 되어 드리겠습니다.

don't tips
꼭 공유하고 싶었습니다.

Don't be afraid of making mistakes.
틀리는 것을 두려워 하지 마세요.

Don't be too ashamed to speak.
말하는 것을 창피해 하지 마세요.

틀릴수록 더 잘 배웁니다. 오류를 범하지 않고 완벽한 영어를 구사하고 싶다면
영어로 말하는 것을 포기하세요. 원어민들도 오류를 범합니다.
유창하게 영어로 말하는 것은 시간과 노력이 필요합니다. 틀려도 오늘부터 무조건 말하세요!
영어를 배우려면 입을 열어 말하면 됩니다.
단어를 많이 모르고 문법이 약하다는 핑계는 **여기서 stop!**

Don't stop listening and repeating.
듣고 따라 하기를 멈추지 마세요.

듣고 또 듣다 보면 어느 순간 갑자기 귀가 열리면서 말문이 터지기 시작합니다.
말하기의 가장 빠른 길은 많이 듣고 열심히 따라 하기 입니다.

Don't get frustrated with yourself.
스스로 좌절하지 마세요.

한국말처럼 표현할 수 없다고 해서 절대로 좌절하지 마세요.
적절한 어휘가 생각나지 않아 낙담하는 경우도 있겠지만
이런 좌절은 영어를 습득하는 데 있어서 꼭 거쳐야 하는 과정입니다.
해결방법은 정말 간단합니다. 연습! 연습! 또 연습!

Don't take it personally when people don't understand you.
내가 영어로 이야기 했는데 상대방이 이해 못했다고 속상해 하지 마세요.

사람마다 억양이 다르기 때문에 말하는 내가 문제가 아니라 못 알아듣는 상대방 문제일 경우도
있습니다. 예를 들어서 미국에서 유학한 사람도 영국인과의 대화가 어려울 때가 있으니까요.

Don't compare yourself to other English speakers.
유창하게 영어를 하는 사람과의 비교는 금물입니다.

모든 사람이 다르듯 언어를 습득하고 활용하는 능력도 다릅니다.
굳이 비교하면서 슬퍼하거나 멈추지 마세요.
프레그마틱 토크와 함께하고 있는 여러분은 이미 반은 성공한 겁니다.
머지않아 해외여행, 비즈니스 출장이 기다려지는 그날까지

프레그마틱 토크와 함께 GO GO~

I've missed more than 9000 shots in my career. I've lost almost 300 games. 26 times, I've been trusted to take the game winning shot and missed. I've failed over and over and over again in my life. And that is why I succeed.

– Michael Jordan

SPECIAL THANKS TO

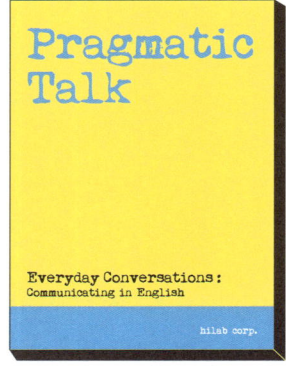 실생활편

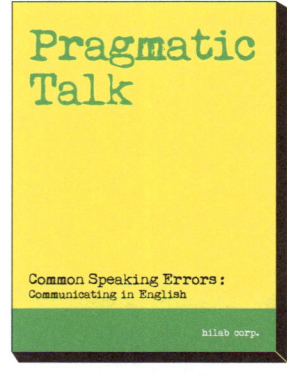 오류잡기편

 은어·숙어편

이 책이 나오기까지 길잡이 역할을 해주신 정용수 사장님, 조언을 아끼지 않으신 홍서진 본부장님, 장충상 전무님, 김동명 상무님, 윤석오 실장님 감사드립니다.

본 콘텐츠를 적용하고 피드백을 허락해 주신 Texas A&M University에 L.Q. Dixon 교수님과 참여해 주신 대학원생 Solbee Kim, Jeong Hyun Park, Haemin Kim, Zihan Geng 그리고 Shuang Wu님 감사드립니다.

프레그마틱 토크가 나오길 기다려 주시고 관심을 가져주신 숙명여자대학교 28기 DO WELL 선생님들, 원우회 선생님들, 그리고 롤모델 홍수잔대표님 감사드립니다.

이 책의 시작부터 마무리까지 함께해주신 하이랩 패밀리 멤버 Joe, R cky, Steve 감사드립니다.

FEATURES

> Hello.
> This is Joe.

안녕하세요.
여러분의 1:1 튜터 조우입니다.

Texas A&M 대학원에서 교육학석사를 받았으며 영어가 모국어가 아닌 사람들을 대상으로 하는 영어교수법과 커리큘럼 설계에 대한 연구를 하였습니다. 영어로 프리토킹이 가능한 그날까지 조우가 함께 하겠습니다.

Pragmatic Talk의 특징

(1) 영어는 영어로 배우자!
　원어민의 말을 반복해서 듣고 또 듣다 보면 귀가 열립니다.
　그리고 머지않아 입이 열리게 됩니다.

(2) 대화 플로우를 알면 게임 끝!
　언제, 어떻게, 무엇을 말해야 하는지 방법을 알면 영어는 쉬워집니다.

> **Texas A&M** 대학원에 재학중인 ESL 학생들에게 적용, 효율적인 학습방법 검증

Pragmatic Talk(실생활편)의 특징

LISTEN to as much English as possible.
220편의 저자직강 강의 동영상과 MP4음성파일이 수록되어 있습니다.
반복해서 원어민 강의를 듣고 따라 하면 대화 흐름과 패턴을 자연스럽게 체득하게 됩니다.

READ as much English as possible.
읽기를 통해 어휘, 문장 표현 능력을 키워줍니다.

SPEAK with natives.
미쿡(^^) 친구 조우가 당신의 1:1 튜터가 되겠습니다.

FEATURES

1. INTRODUCTION
원어민 튜터 조우의 음성으로 주제에 대한 목표 알기

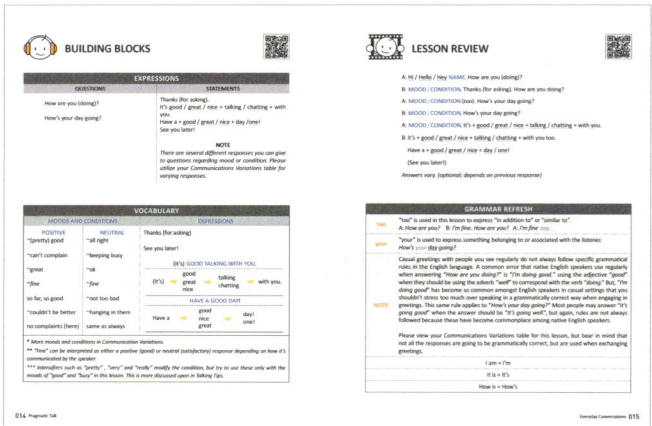

2. BUILDING BLOCKS
주제에 대한 표현과 단어를 듣고 학습 준비하기

3. LESSON REVIEW
동영상 강의 플레이로 주제에 대한 핵심알기

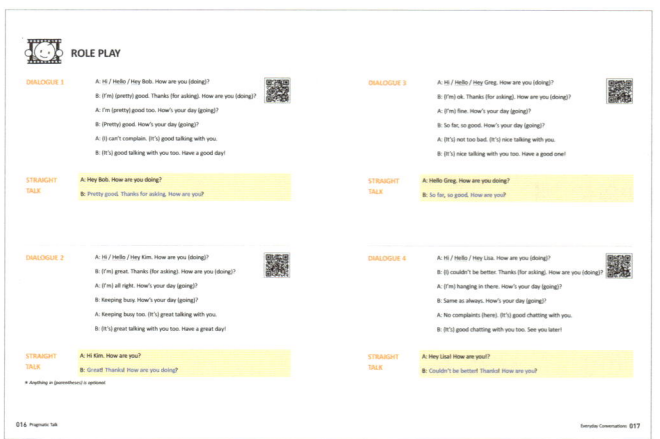

4. ROLE PLAY
일대일 동영상을 통해 롤플레이 회화문 연습하기

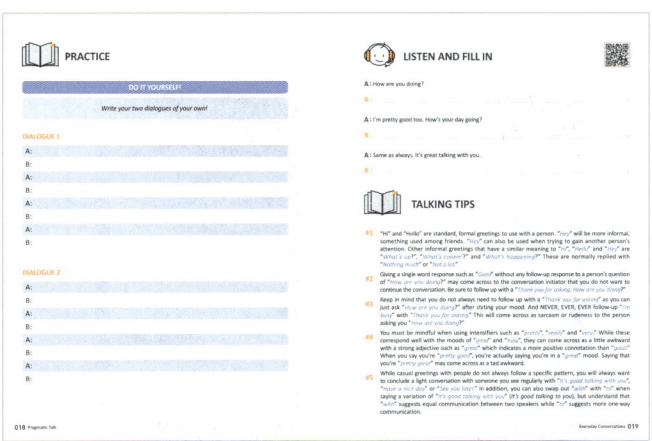

5. PRACTICE
나만의 대화 문장 만들어 보기

6. LISTEN AND FILL IN
음성을 듣고 받아쓰기

7. TALKING TIPS
원어민이 알려주는 대화할 때 유용한 정보 및 핵심 팁 알기

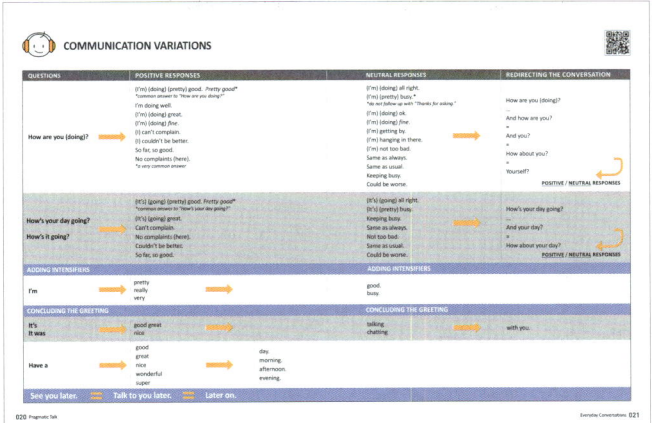

8. COMMUICATION VARIATIONS
플로우 차트를 보고 들으며 대화의 흐름알기

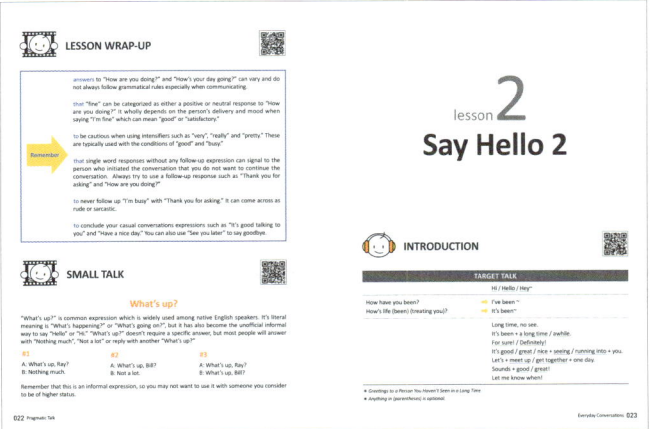

9. LESSON WRAP-UP
학습 마무리 동영상 보기

10. SMALL TALK
조우가 들려드리는 미쿡(?) 잡담 이야기 듣기

ATTENTION

원어민 저자 직강 동영상 & MP4 음원 보고 듣는 방법

QR코드 어플 다운방법

① 플레이스토어로 들어간다. ② 검색창에 "큐알코드" 라고 입력한다. ③ 어플을 선택한다. ④ 설치 버튼을 누른다.

웹사이트에서 바로보기

1. URL 입력 : https://www.youtube.com/channel/UC-S4N2ec_vuljy63c2QW06A

2. 유튜브 검색창에 **"하이랩"** 검색

프톡과 1:1 대화창 개설 방법

카카오 옐로페이지 친구 추가에서 "@프레그마틱 토크"를 검색하여 추가한다.

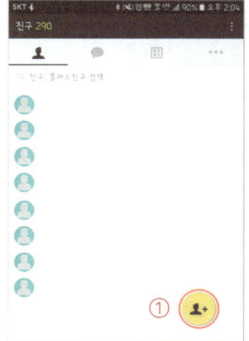 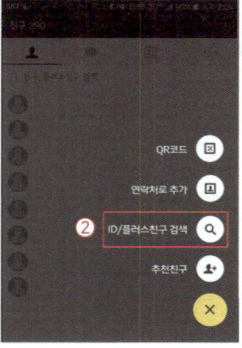 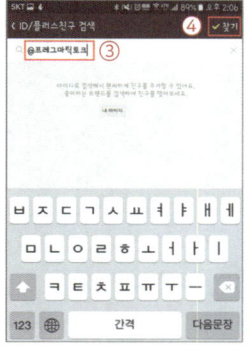 

MP4 음원파일 다운받는 방법

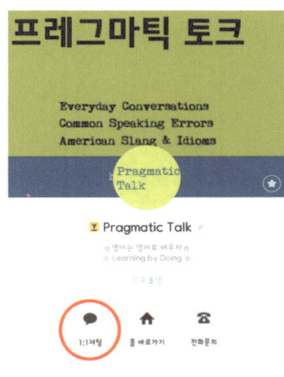 

카카오 옐로페이지에서
@프레그마틱 토크 친구 추가 후
문의바람

네이버 QR코드 리딩방법

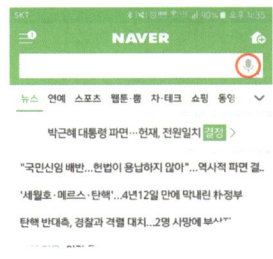 

다음 QR코드 리딩방법

CONTENTS

Everyday Conversations
: 실생활편

SECTION 01 | DAILY LIFE

LESSON 1	Say Hello 1	013
LESSON 2	Say Hello 2	023
LESSON 3	Replying to Negative Responses	035
LESSON 4	Shopping for Clothes	045
LESSON 5	Exchanges and Refunds	057
LESSON 6	At the Hair Salon	067
LESSON 7	At the Cafe	077

SECTION 02 | MY LIFE

LESSON 8	Basic Introductions	089
LESSON 9	Tell Me About Your Family 1	099
LESSON 10	Tell Me About Your Family 2	111
LESSON 11	Tell Me About Your Best Friend	123
LESSON 12	Talking About Hobbies	135
LESSON 13	My Favorite Things	147
LESSON 14	Making an Appointment with a Friend	159

SECTION 03 | FREE TIME

LESSON 15	Eating Out 1	173
LESSON 16	Eating Out 2 Ordering Fast Food	183
LESSON 17	Out for Drinks	195
LESSON 18	Plans for the Weekend	205
LESSON 19	Somewhere to Travel	215
LESSON 20	At the Airport: Customs and Immigration	225

SECTION

1

DAILY LIFE

*"To learn something new,
you need to try new things and not be afraid to be wrong."*

Roy T. Bennett

lesson 1
Say Hello 1

 **INTRODUCTION**

TARGET TALK
Hi / Hello / Hey
How are you (doing)?   →   (I'm)~   How's your day (going)?   →   (It's)~
(Thanks (for asking)).   (It's) good / great / nice + talking / chatting + with you.   Have a + good / great / nice + day / one!   See you later!

* *Greetings to a Person You See Regularly.*
* *Anything in (parentheses) is optional.*

 # BUILDING BLOCKS

EXPRESSIONS

QUESTIONS	STATEMENTS
How are you (doing)? How's your day going?	Thanks (for asking). It's <u>good</u> / <u>great</u> / <u>nice</u> + <u>talking</u> / <u>chatting</u> + with you. Have a + <u>good</u> / <u>great</u> / <u>nice</u> + <u>day</u> /<u>one</u>! See you later!

NOTE

There are several different responses you can give to questions regarding mood or condition. Please utilize your Communications Variations table for varying responses.

VOCABULARY

MOODS AND CONDITIONS

POSITIVE	NEUTRAL
~(pretty) good	~all right
~can't complain	~keeping busy
~great	~ok
~*fine*	~*fine*
so far, so good	~not too bad
~couldn't be better	~hanging in there
no complaints (here)	same as always

EXPRESSIONS

Thanks (for asking)

See you later!

(It's) **GOOD TALKING WITH YOU.**

(It's) → good / great / nice → talking / chatting → with you.

HAVE A GOOD DAY!

Have a → good / nice / great → day! / one!

---

* More moods and conditions in Communication Variations.

** "Fine" can be interpreted as either a positive (good) or neutral (satisfactory) response depending on how it's communicated by the speaker.

*** Intensifiers such as "pretty", "very" and "really" modify the condition, but try to use these only with the moods of "good" and "busy" in this lesson. This is more discussed upon in Talking Tips.

LESSON REVIEW

A: <u>Hi</u> / <u>Hello</u> / <u>Hey</u> **NAME**. How are you (doing)?

B: **MOOD/CONDITION**. Thanks (for asking). How are you doing?

A: **MOOD/CONDITION** (*too*). How's your day going?

B: **MOOD/CONDITION**. How's your day going?

A: **MOOD/CONDITION**. It's + <u>good</u> / <u>great</u> / <u>nice</u> + <u>talking</u> / <u>chatting</u> + with you.

B: It's + <u>good</u> / <u>great</u> / <u>nice</u> + <u>talking</u> / <u>chatting</u> + with you too.

Have a + <u>good</u> / <u>great</u> / <u>nice</u> + <u>day</u> / <u>one</u>!

(See you later!)

Answers vary. (optional; depends on previous response)

	GRAMMAR REFRESH
too	"too" is used in this lesson to express "in addition to" or "similar to". A: *How are you?* B: *I'm fine. How are you?* A: *I'm fine too.*
your	"your" is used to express something belonging to or associated with the listener. *How's your day going?*
NOTE	Casual greetings with people you see regularly do not always follow specific grammatical rules in the English language. A common error that native English speakers use regularly when answering *"How are you doing?"* is *"I'm doing good."* using the adjective *"good"* when they should be using the adverb *"well"* to correspond with the verb *"doing."* But, *"I'm doing good"* has become so common amongst English speakers in casual settings that you shouldn't stress too much over speaking in a grammatically correct way when engaging in greetings. This same rule applies to *"How's your day going?"* Most people may answer *"It's going good"* when the answer should be *"It's going well."*, but again, rules are not always followed because these have become commonplace among native English speakers. Please view your Communications Variations table for this lesson, but bear in mind that not all the responses are going to be grammatically correct, but are used when exchanging greetings.
	I am = I'm
	It is = It's
	How is = How's

Everyday Conversations

# ROLE PLAY

DIALOGUE 1

A: <u>Hi</u> / <u>Hello</u> / <u>Hey</u> Bob. How are you (doing)?

B: (I'm) (pretty) good. Thanks (for asking). How are you (doing)?

A: I'm (pretty) good too. How's your day (going)?

B: (Pretty) good. How's your day (going)?

A: (I) can't complain. (It's) good talking with you.

B: (It's) good talking with you too. Have a good day!

STRAIGHT TALK

A: Hey Bob. How are you doing?

B: **Pretty good. Thanks for asking. How are you**?

DIALOGUE 2

A: <u>Hi</u> / <u>Hello</u> / <u>Hey</u> Kim. How are you (doing)?

B: (I'm) great. Thanks (for asking). How are you (doing)?

A: (I'm) all right. How's your day (going)?

B: Keeping busy. How's your day (going)?

A: Keeping busy too. (It's) great talking with you.

B: (It's) great talking with you too. Have a great day!

STRAIGHT TALK

A: Hi Kim. How are you?

B: **Great! Thanks! How are you doing**?

∗ *Anything in (parentheses) is optional.*

DIALOGUE 3

A: Hi / Hello / Hey Greg. How are you (doing)?

B: (I'm) ok. Thanks (for asking). How are you (doing)?

A: (I'm) fine. How's your day (going)?

B: So far, so good. How's your day (going)?

A: (It's) not too bad. (It's) nice talking with you.

B: (It's) nice talking with you too. Have a good one!

STRAIGHT TALK

A: Hello Greg. How are you doing?

B: So far, so good. How are you?

DIALOGUE 4

A: Hi / Hello / Hey Lisa. How are you (doing)?

B: (I) couldn't be better. Thanks (for asking). How are you (doing)?

A: (I'm) hanging in there. How's your day (going)?

B: Same as always. How's your day (going)?

A: No complaints (here). (It's) good chatting with you.

B: (It's) good chatting with you too. See you later!

STRAIGHT TALK

A: Hey Lisa! How are you!?

B: Couldn't be better! Thanks! How are you?

Everyday Conversations 017

PRACTICE

DO IT YOURSELF!

Write your two dialogues of your own!

DIALOGUE 1

A:
B:
A:
B:
A:
B:
A:
B:

DIALOGUE 2

A:
B:
A:
B:
A:
B:
A:
B:

 # LISTEN AND FILL IN

A : How are you doing?

B : _____ .

A : I'm pretty good too. How's your day going?

B : _____ .

A : Same as always. It's great talking with you.

B : _____ .

 # TALKING TIPS

#1 "Hi" and "Hello" are standard, formal greetings to use with a person. "*Hey*" will be more informal, something used among friends. "*Hey*" can also be used when trying to gain another person's attention. Other informal greetings that have a similar meaning to "*Hi*", "*Hello*" and "*Hey*" are "*What's up*?", "*What's cookin'*?" and "*What's happening*?" These are normally replied with "*Nothing much*" or "*Not a lot.*"

#2 Giving a single word response such as "*Good*" without any follow-up response to a person's question of "*How are you doing*?" may come across to the conversation initiator that you do not want to continue the conversation. Be sure to follow up with a "*Thank you for asking. How are you doing*?"

#3 Keep in mind that you do not always need to follow up with a "*Thank you for asking*" as you can just ask "*How are you doing*?" after stating your mood. And NEVER, EVER, EVER follow-up "*I'm busy*" with "*Thank you for asking.*" This will come across as sarcasm or rudeness to the person asking you "*How are you doing*?"

#4 You must be mindful when using intensifiers such as "*pretty*", "*really*" and "*very.*" While these correspond well with the moods of "*good*" and "*busy*", they can come across as a little awkward with a strong adjective such as "*great*" which indicates a more positive connotation than "*good.*" When you say you're "*pretty good*", you're actually saying you're in a "*great*" mood. Saying that you're "*pretty great*" may come across as a tad awkward.

#5 While casual greetings with people do not always follow a specific pattern, you will always want to conclude a light conversation with someone you see regularly with "*It's good talking with you*", "*Have a nice day*" or "*See you later.*" In addition, you can also swap out "*with*" with "*to*" when saying a variation of "*It's good talking with you*" (*It's good talking to you*), but understand that "*with*" suggests equal communication between two speakers while "*to*" suggests more one-way communication.

COMMUNICATION VARIATIONS

QUESTIONS	POSITIVE RESPONSES
How are you (doing)?	(I'm) (doing) (pretty) good. *Pretty good** **common answer to "How are you doing?"* I'm doing well. (I'm) (doing) great. (I'm) (doing) *fine*. (I) can't complain. (I) couldn't be better. So far, so good. No complaints (here). **a very common answer*
How's your day going? How's it going?	(It's) (going) (pretty) good. *Pretty good** **common answer to "How's your day going?"* (It's) (going) great. Can't complain. No complaints (here). Couldn't be better. So far, so good.

ADDING INTENSIFIERS

| I'm | → | pretty <br> really <br> very | → | |

CONCLUDING THE GREETING

| It's
 It was | → | good great <br> nice | → | |
| Have a | → | good <br> great <br> nice <br> wonderful <br> super | → | day.
 morning.
 afternoon.
 evening. |

See you later. = **Talk to you later.** = **Later on.**

NEUTRAL RESPONSES

(I'm) (doing) all right.
(I'm) (pretty) busy.*
*do not follow up with "Thanks for asking."
(I'm) (doing) ok.
(I'm) (doing) *fine*.
(I'm) getting by.
(I'm) hanging in there.
(I'm) not too bad.
Same as always.
Same as usual.
Keeping busy.
Could be worse.

REDIRECTING THE CONVERSATION

How are you (doing)?
...
And how are you?
=
And you?
=
How about you?
=
Yourself?

POSITIVE / **NEUTRAL** RESPONSES

(It's) (going) all right.
(It's) (pretty) busy.
Keeping busy.
Same as always.
Not too bad.
Same as usual.
Could be worse.

How's your day going?
...
And your day?
=
How about your day?

POSITIVE / **NEUTRAL** RESPONSES

ADDING INTENSIFIERS

good.
busy.

CONCLUDING THE GREETING

talking
chatting

with you.

Everyday Conversations **021**

 # LESSON WRAP-UP

> **Remember**
>
> **answers** to "How are you doing?" and "How's your day going?" can vary and do not always follow grammatical rules especially when communicating.
>
> **that** "fine" can be categorized as either a positive or neutral response to "How are you doing?" It wholly depends on the person's delivery and mood when saying "I'm fine" which can mean "good" or "satisfactory."
>
> **to** be cautious when using intensifiers such as "very", "really" and "pretty." These are typically used with the conditions of "good" and "busy."
>
> **that** single word responses without any follow-up expression can signal to the person who initiated the conversation that you do not want to continue the conversation. Always try to use a follow-up response such as "Thank you for asking" and "How are you doing?"
>
> **to** never follow up "I'm busy" with "Thank you for asking." It can come across as rude or sarcastic.
>
> **to** conclude your casual conversations expressions such as "It's good talking to you" and "Have a nice day." You can also use "See you later" to say goodbye.

 # SMALL TALK

What's up?

"What's up?" is common expression which is widely used among native English speakers. It's literal meaning is "What's happening?" or "What's going on?", but it has also become the unofficial informal way to say "Hello" or "Hi." "What's up?" doesn't require a specific answer, but most people will answer with "Nothing much", "Not a lot" or reply with another "What's up?"

#1
A: What's up, Ray?
B: Nothing much.

#2
A: What's up, Bill?
B: Not a lot.

#3
A: What's up, Ray?
B: What's up, Bill?

Remember that this is an informal expression, so you may not want to use it with someone you consider to be of higher status.

lesson 2
Say Hello 2

 **INTRODUCTION**

TARGET TALK	
	Hi / Hello / Hey~
How have you been? How's life (been) (treating you)?	➡ I've been ~ ➡ It's been~
	Long time, no see. It's been + a long time / awhile. For sure! / Definitely! It's good / great / nice + seeing / running into + you. Let's + meet up / get together + one day. Sounds + good / great! Let me know when!

∗ *Greetings to a Person You Haven't Seen in a Long Time.*
∗ *Anything in (parentheses) is optional.*

BUILDING BLOCKS

EXPRESSIONS

QUESTIONS	STATEMENTS
How have you been? How's life (been) (treating you)?	Long time, no see. It's been + a long time / awhile. For sure! / Definitely! It's good / great / nice + seeing / running into + you. Let's + meet up / get together + one day. Sounds + good / great! Let me know when!

NOTE

Like Say Hello 1, there are several different responses you can give to questions regarding mood or condition in regards to a person you haven't seen in a long time. Please utilize your Communications Variations table for varying responses.

VOCABULARY

MOODS AND CONDITIONS

POSITIVE	NEUTRAL
~(pretty) good	~all right
(I) can't complain.	(It's) keeping me busy.
~great	~ok
~well	~not too bad
(I) couldn't be better.	(I'm) hanging in there.
No complaints here.	Same as always.

OTHER EXPRESSIONS

EXPRESSIONS OF TIME

Long time, no see!

It's been → a long time! / awhile!

PLEASANTRIES

It's → good / great / nice → seeing you! / running into you!

ACKNOWLEDGEMENTS

For sure!
Definitely!
Sounds good / great!

ADDITIONAL EXPRESSIONS

Let's meet up one day!
Let's get together one day!
Let me know when!

 # LESSON REVIEW

A: <u>Hi</u> / <u>Hello</u> / <u>Hey</u> **NAME**. **EXPRESSION OF TIME**.
B: **ACKNOWLEDGEMENT OF TIME EXPRESSION**. **EXPRESSION OF TIME**.
   How have you been?
A: **MOOD / CONDITION**. How have you been?
B: **MOOD / CONDITION** *(too)*. How's life (been) (treating you)?
A: **MOOD / CONDITION**. How's life (been) treating you?
B: **MOOD / CONDITION** *(too)*. It's <u>good</u> / <u>great</u> / <u>nice</u> + <u>seeing</u> / <u>running into</u> + you.
A: It's <u>good</u> / <u>great</u> / <u>nice</u> + <u>seeing</u> / <u>running into</u> + you too.
   Let's + <u>meet up</u> / <u>get together</u> + one day.
B: Sounds + <u>good</u> / <u>great</u>! Let me know when!

Answers vary. (optional; depends on previous response)

	GRAMMAR REFRESH
too	"too" is used in this lesson to express "in addition to" or "similar to". A: *How have you been?* B: *I've been great. How have you been?* A: *I've been great* too.
again	"again" is used to express the meaning "once more." Use this at the end of the expression "It's nice to see you" as it indicates you are seeing or once more talking with a friend that you used to see or visit regularly. Do not use it with "It's nice running into you." "Run into" means to "collide with" but in the expression "It's nice running into you" means that you've had an unexpected encounter with someone from your past. *It's nice seeing you* again*!*
past participle (been)	"been" is the past participle of "be" and in this lesson it's serving the purpose of asking for or stating how one's condition has been in the past and the present.
NOTE	This lesson is similar to Say Hello 1 in that the responses to the questions tend to be informal in spoken conversation and do not always follow a specific pattern or proper grammatical rules. Please utilize your Communication Variation table and Talking Tips section for further ways to communicate with a friend you haven't seen in a long time.
	<u>I have</u> = <u>I've</u> ; <u>I am</u> = <u>I'm</u>
	<u>It has</u> = <u>It's</u> been a long time. / <u>It is</u> = <u>It's</u> good seeing you.

Everyday Conversations **025**

 # ROLE PLAY

DIALOGUE 1

A: Hi / Hello / Hey Randy. Long time, no see!

B: For sure! (It's) been a long time! How have you been?

A: ((I've) been) pretty good. How have you been?

B: ((I've) been) (pretty) good too. How's life (been) (treating you)?

A: ((It's) been) (pretty) good. How's life (been) treating you?

B: (I) can't complain. (It's) good seeing you (again).

A: (It's) good seeing you too. Let's meet up one day!

B: Sounds good! Let me know when!

STRAIGHT TALK

A: Hey Randy! Long time, no see!

B: **For sure! Good seeing you! How have you been**?

DIALOGUE 2

A: Hi / Hello / Hey Ted. It's been a long time!

B: Definitely! (It's) been awhile. How have you been?

A: ((I've) been) great. How have you been?

B: (I've been) all right. How's life (been) (treating you)?

A: (It's been) keeping me busy. How's life (been) treating you?

B: (It's been) keeping me busy too. (It's) great running into you.

A: (It's) great running into you too. Let's get together one day!

B: Sounds great! Let me know when!

STRAIGHT TALK

A: Hi Ted! How have you been?

B: **Been great! It's been awhile! How have you been**?

* *Anything in (parentheses) is optional.*

DIALOGUE 3

A: Hi / Hello / Hey Betty. Long time, no see!

B: For sure! (It's) been a long time! How have you been?

A: ((I've) been) ok. How have you been?

B: ((I've) been doing) well. How's life (been) (treating you)?

A: (It's) (been) treating me well. How's life (been) treating you?

B: Not too bad. (It's) nice seeing you (again).

A: (It's) nice seeing you too. Let's meet up one day!

B: Sounds good! Let me know when!

STRAIGHT TALK

A: Hello Betty! Long time, no see! How have you been?

B: **Been ok. Not too bad. How's life been treating you**?

DIALOGUE 4

A: Hi / Hello / Hey Lisa. It's been awhile!

B: Definitely! Long time, no see! How have you been?

A: (I) couldn't be better. How have you been?

B: (I'm) hanging in there. How's life (been) (treating you)?

A: Same as always. How's life (been) treating you?

B: No complaints (here). (It's) good running into you!

A: (It's) good running into you too. Let's get together one day!

B: Sounds good! Let me know when!

STRAIGHT TALK

A: Hey Lisa! It's been awhile! How have you been?

B: **Definitely! Couldn't be better! How have you been**?

PRACTICE

DO IT YOURSELF!

Write your two dialogues of your own!

DIALOGUE 1

A:
B:
A:
B:
A:
B:
A:
B:

DIALOGUE 2

A:
B:
A:
B:
A:
B:
A:
B:

 **LISTEN AND FILL IN**

A: Hey Tom! Long time, no see!

B: _____.

A: Been pretty good. How have you been?

B: _____.

A: Same as always. How's life been treating you?

B: _____.

A: It's great seeing you too! Let's meet up one day!

B: _____.

 **TALKING TIPS**

Exchanging greetings with someone you haven't seen in a long time can be tricky especially when it comes to the appropriate response to their statement. Greetings in general are flexible and do not always follow specific patterns or grammatical rules. But, there are exceptions. Please view the tips below to gain a better understanding of how communication works when greeting someone you haven't seen in a long time.

Continued on next page ➡

#1 Most people you haven't seen in a long time will approach you with an expression related to the extended period of time they haven't seen you. Here, you'll want to respond by acknowledging the expression of time and produce one of your own if you want. You can then follow that up with "*How have you been?*" or the person who initiated the conversation will ask "*How have you been?*" View the chart below for this situation.

SITUATION A	SITUATION B
Pattern	**Pattern**
A: Hey NAME! EXPRESSIONS OF TIME! B: ACKNOWLEDGEMENT! (EXPRESSIONS OF TIME!) How have you been?	A: Hey NAME! EXPRESSIONS OF TIME! B: ACKNOWLEDGEMENT. (EXPRESSIONS OF TIME!) A: How have you been?
Example	**Example**
A: Hey, Amy! Long time, no see! B: For sure! (Long time, no see!) How have you been?	A: Hey, Amy! It's been a long time! B: Definitely! (Long time, no see!) A: How have you been?

#2 From this point forward, you'll want to respond to the last item spoken by the person beginning the conversation. If they use the expression "*It's good to see you*" as the final part of their greeting you should respond to that expression first. If they ask "*How have you been?*" as the final part of the greeting, answer the question "*How have you been?*" You can follow both of these up with a redirect of "*How have you been?*" View the chart below for this situation.

SITUATION A	SITUATION B
Pattern	**Pattern**

A: Hey NAME! EXPRESSIONS OF TIME!
   It's good to see you.
B: It's good to see you too!
   How have you been?
	A: Hey NAME! EXPRESSIONS OF TIME!
	   How have you been?
	B: MOOD/CONDITION. How have you been?

Example	**Example**

A: Hey, Amy! Long time no see!
   It's good to see you!
B: It's good to see you too!
   How have you been?
	A: Hey, Amy! It's been a long time!
	   How have you been?
	B: I've been great! How have you been?

#3 Then there will be the rare situation where someone you haven't seen in a long time gives you a long, extended greeting. This usually happens when a person is REALLY excited to see you. They may greet you with "*Hi*" follow it up with an expression of time, a pleasantry and "*How have you been*?" In this situation, first respond to the pleasantry, then answer your mood/condition and finally ask the person "*How have you been*?" View the table below for this situation.

SITUATION
Pattern
A: Hey NAME! EXPRESSIONS OF TIME! PLEASANTRY! How have you been!?   B: PLEASANTRY too! MOOD/CONDITION! How have you been!?
Example
A: Hey, Amy! Long time, no see! It's good to see you! How have you been!?   B: It's good to see you too! I've been all right. How have you been!?

#4 If someone asks you "*How's life been treating you*?" or one of its abbreviated forms such as "*How's life*?" you must always must redirect it using the full question: "*How's life (been) treating you*?" Don't redirect with the abbreviated form of the question as it will come across as awkward. View the table below for this situation.

SITUATION A	SITUATION B	SITUATION C
A: How's life?	A: How's life been?	A: How's life been treating you?
B: Been good. How's life (been) treating you?	B: Been good. How's life (been) treating you?	B: Been good. How's life (been) treating you?

#5 Usually a conversation between two people who enjoy each other's company will end in a request to meet up one day in the future. Be sure to use "*one day*" at the end of "*Let's meet up*" or "*Let's get together*" as it indicates an unknown near future time. When someone requests to "*meet up*" or "*get together*" be sure to affirm their request with "*Sounds great / good*!" as stating this indicates that you are willing and looking forward to meeting that person at a later date. Then follow it with "*Let me know when*!"

#6 The same rules apply in this lesson as they do when providing responses to the question "*How have you been*?" Single one-word answers without any extension in the conversation or without re-directing questions asked may indicate to the listener that you do not want to continue the conversation.

COMMUNICATION VARIATIONS

QUESTIONS	POSITIVE RESPONSES
How have you been?	Pretty good* *common answer ((I've) been) (pretty) good. (I'm) (pretty) good. (I've) been doing well. ((I've) been) great. I can't complain. I couldn't be better. No complaints here.
How's life (been) (treating you)?	Pretty good.* *common answer. (It's) (been) (treating me) (pretty) good. (It's) (been) (treating me) great. I can't complain. No complaints (here). (It) couldn't be better. So far, so good.

OTHER EXPRESSIONS OF TIME

It's been ages!

I haven't seen you in a blue moon!

OTHER ACKNOWLEDGEMENTS

Absolutely!
You're not kidding!
(Yes), indeed!

* "Fine" can be interpreted as a "good" or "neutral" condition.

NEUTRAL RESPONSES	REDIRECTING THE CONVERSATION
((I've) been) all right. ((I've) been) busy. ((I've) been) ok. ((I've) been) getting by. (I'm) getting by. ((I've) been) hanging in there. (I'm) hanging in there. (I'm) not too bad. Same as always. Same as usual. (I'm) keeping busy. Could be worse.	(And) how have you been? = And you? = Yourself? = How about you? = Tell me how you've been. **POSITIVE** / **NEUTRAL** RESPONSES
(It's) (been) all right. (It's) (been) (keeping me) busy. (It's been) ok. ((I've) been) hanging in there. (I'm) hanging in there. ((I've) been) getting by. (I'm) getting by. (It's) not too bad. Same as always. Same as usual. (It) could be worse.	(And) how's life (been) treating you? = (And) how's life been for you? = And you? = Yourself? = How about you? **POSITIVE** / **NEUTRAL** RESPONSES

OTHER PLEASANTRIES

It's → great / good / nice → bumping into you!

OTHER AFFIRMATIONS

Sounds like a plan!
Sure, I'd like that!

 # LESSON WRAP-UP

Remember

that answers to "How have you been?" are prone to flexibility and do not always follow grammatical rules especially when in communicative form.

to follow the patterns discussed upon in Talking Tips. There are certain rules and guidelines to follow when it comes to communicating with a person you haven't seen in a long time.

to ensure that the communication doesn't come across as awkward.

to end a brief conversation with someone you haven't seen in a long time, by offering to meet up with them one day.

 # SMALL TALK

Once In a Blue Moon

(Once) in a blue moon is an idiom which expresses a long period of time. The literal meaning of "blue moon" refers to the second full moon in any given month which is quite rare (there are approximately 13 full moons a year). When you see a person you haven't seen in a long time, you can greet them with "I haven't seen you in a blue moon!" Also, when you're asked about a person you haven't seen in a long time (Have you seen him / her?) or the frequency in which you see that person (How often do you see him / her?), you can also use the blue moon idiom.

Have you seen him / her? I haven't seen him / her in a blue moon.

How often do you see him / her? I see him / her once in a blue moon.

lesson 3
Replying to Negative Responses

 **INTRODUCTION**

TARGET TALK		
How are you (doing)?	➡	Hi / Hello / Hey
What's wrong?	➡	(I'm) (feeling)~ You should~
	I have a~ I'm <u>sorry</u> / <u>hate</u> to hear that. <u>I'm planning on it.</u> / <u>I intend to</u>. If there's anything I can do, just let me know I'll be <u>ok</u> / <u>all right</u>. <u>Thank you for your concern.</u> / <u>I appreciate your concern</u>.	

* *Anything in (parentheses) is optional.*

Everyday Conversations

 # BUILDING BLOCKS

EXPRESSIONS

QUESTIONS	STATEMENTS
How are you doing? What's wrong?	I'm <u>sorry</u> / <u>hate</u> to hear that. I'm <u>planning on it</u>. / <u>I intend to</u>. If there's anything I can do, just let me know I'll be <u>ok</u> / <u>all right</u>. <u>Thank you for your concern</u>. / <u>I appreciate your concern</u>.

NOTE
There are several different responses you can give to questions in this lesson. Please utilize your Communications Variations table for varying responses.

VOCABULARY

NEGATIVE CONDITIONS	EXPRESSIONS		
	EXPRESSIONS OF SYMPATHY		
(I'm) not too good.	I'm sorry I hate	➡	to hear that.
(I'm) stressed out.	**ADVICE**		
I could be better.	You should	➡	take a vacation. get some rest. take some medicine. (go) see a doctor.
(I'm) (feeling) burned out.			
(I'm) (feeling) terrible.	**DECLARATIVE STATEMENTS**		
(I'm) (feeling) under the weather.	I'm planning on it. I intend to. I'll be <u>ok</u> / <u>all right</u>.		
	EXPRESSIONS OF SUPPORT		
	If there's anything I can, just let me know. I hope you feel better soon.		
	EXPRESSIONS OF GRATITUDE		
	Thank you for your concern. I appreciate your concern.		

INTENSIFIERS	ADJECTIVES	ACHES	EXCLAMATIONS
so	terrible bad	headache stomachache	Oh, no!

 # LESSON REVIEW

A: Hi / Hello / Hey **NAME**. How are you (doing)?

B: **NEGATIVE CONDITION**.

A: What's wrong?

B: **NEGATIVE CONDITION**. / I have a **ACHE**.

A: You should **ADVICE**.

B: I'm planning on it. / I intend to.

A: If there's anything I can do, just let me know. / (I) hope you feel better soon.

B: I'll be ok / all right. **EXPRESSION OF GRATITUDE**.

GRAMMAR REFRESH	
NOTE	Take into account that this lesson, like Say Hello 1 and Say Hello 2, will not strictly follow grammatical rules due to the flexibility presented within the context of exchanging greetings and responding to individuals who reply with negative responses.
should	"should" is a modal verb which is used to express a duty or an obligation. It's most often used when giving another person advice. You *should* see a doctor.
anything	"anything" is used, to refer to "a thing" no matter what it is. If there's *anything* I can do, just let me know.
can	"can" is a modal verb used to express ability. If there's anything I *can* do, just let me know.
do	"do" means to perform a general action. If there's anything I can *do*...
just	"just" is used in this lesson as a polite way to give permission. ...*just* let me know.
soon	"soon" is an adverb which means "in a short time." I *hope* you feel better soon.

Everyday Conversations

ROLE PLAY

DIALOGUE 1

A: Hi / Hello / Hey Jennifer. How are you (doing)?

B: (I'm) not too good.

A: What's wrong?

B: (I'm) (so) stressed out.

A: (Oh, no). I'm sorry to hear that. You should take a vacation.

A: I'm planning on it.

B: If there's anything I can do, just let me know.

A: I'll be ok. Thank you for your concern.

STRAIGHT TALK

A: Hi Jennifer. How are you?

B: **Not too good. So stressed out.**

DIALOGUE 2

A: Hi / Hello / Hey Tom. How are you (doing)?

B: (I) could be better.

A: What's wrong?

B: (I'm) (feeling) burned out.

A: (Oh, no). I hate to hear that. You should get some rest.

B: I intend to.

A: If there's anything I can do, just let me know.

B: I'll be all right. I appreciate your concern.

STRAIGHT TALK

A: I could be better. Feeling burned out.

B: **Oh, no. I hate to hear that. You should get some rest.**

DIALOGUE 3

A: Hi / Hello / Hey Jack. How are you (doing)?

B: (I'm feeling) terrible.

A: What's wrong?

B: I have a (bad) headache.

A: (Oh, no). I'm sorry to hear that. You should take some medicine.

B: I'm planning on it.

A: (I) hope you feel better soon.

B: I'll be ok. Thank you for your concern.

STRAIGHT TALK

A: Hi Jack. How are you doing?

B: **I'm feeling terrible. I have a bad headache.**

DIALOGUE 4

A: Hi / Hello / Hey Jerry. How are you (doing)?

B: (I'm feeling) bad.

A: What's wrong?

B: I have a (terrible) stomachache.

A: (Oh, no). I'm sorry to hear that. You should (go) see a doctor.

B: I intend to.

A: (I) hope you feel better soon.

B: I'll be all right. I appreciate your concern.

STRAIGHT TALK

A: I'm feeling bad. I have a terrible stomachache.

B: **Oh, no. I'm sorry to hear that. You should see a doctor.**

Everyday Conversations 039

PRACTICE

DO IT YOURSELF!

Write your two dialogues of your own!

DIALOGUE 1

A:
B:
A:
B:
A:
B:
A:
B:

DIALOGUE 2

A:
B:
A:
B:
A:
B:
A:
B:

 # LISTEN AND FILL IN

A: Hi Jenna. How are you?
B: _____ .
A: What's wrong?
B: _____ .
A: I'm sorry to hear that. You should get some rest.
B: _____ .
A: I hope you feel better soon.
B: _____ .

 # TALKING TIPS

#1 When a person replies with a negative response, he or she may reply with a broad statement like "*not too good*," "*I'm feeling sick*" or "*I'm feeling stressed*." For either response, you can still ask "*What's wrong*?" to gain further, detailed information. Now, if a person replies with "*I'm sick. I have a headache*," there isn't a reason to ask "*What's wrong*?" at this point, since the person has given you a reason (a headache) for why they're feeling sick. It's best at this point to offer an expression of sympathy. View the table below for these two situations.

SITUATION A	SITUATION B
Pattern	**Pattern**
A: Hey Joe. How are you (doing)? B: NEGATIVE CONDITION. A: What's wrong?	A: Hey Joe. How are you doing? B: NEGATIVE CONDITION. I have a ACHE. A: *Exp. of Sympathy*.
Example	**Example**
A: Hey Joe. How are you (doing)? B: I'm stressed out. A: What's wrong?	A: Hey Joe. How are you doing? B: I'm feeling sick. I have a stomachache. A: I'm sorry to hear that.

#2 Use descriptive words like "*bad*" and "*terrible*" to describe an ailment you may have. When someone says "*I have a headache*," the listener will think it's a regular headache. When you say "*I have a bad / terrible headache*," it means you're communicating that you have a headache that is much more severe than the regular headache. You can also use "*a little*" before the "*ache*" you have to describe a minor pain. (I have *a little* headache.)

#3 When you give advice to a person who is not feeling well, give it in concern and try to not come across as too pushy or condescending with it.

#4 Try to give expressions of support to a person who has given you a negative reply before the conversation ends. It will be appreciated and typically the person will provide you a declarative such as "*I'll be all right*." and express gratitude for your concern.

COMMUNICATION VARIATIONS

QUESTIONS	NEGATIVE CONDITIONS
How are you (doing)?	(I'm) not too good / great. (I'm) (feeling) stressed (out). (I'm) (feeling) burned out. I'm feeling terrible / horrible / bad. I'm feeling sick / ill / under the weather. (I) could be better. (I've) been better. (I'm) (feeling) tired / exhausted.
What's wrong?	(I'm) (feeling) stressed (out). (I'm) (feeling) burned out. (I'm) (feeling) sick / ill / under the weather. I have a / an → headache. / stomachache. / toothache. / earache. / backache.

ENHANCING THE NEGATIVE CONDITION WITH INTENSIFIERS AND ADJECTIVES

(I'm) (feeling)	so very super really a little fairly	
I have a	terrible horrible massive small little	

GIVING LIGHT ADVICE

For someone who feels "stressed" or "burned out"	
For someone who feels "sick"	You should →

ENHANCING THE NEGATIVE CONDITION WITH INTENSIFIERS AND ADJECTIVES

stressed (out).
burned (out).
sick / ill.
tired / exhausted.
bad.

headache.
stomachache.
toothache.
earache.
backache.

GIVING LIGHT ADVICE

take a vacation.
get some rest.
take a break.

go see a doctor.
go to the hospital.
take some medicine.
get some rest.

 # LESSON WRAP-UP

Remember

when a person replies with a broad negative response like "not too good" or "I'm stressed", you can ask "What's wrong?" to express concern. Try to refrain from asking "What's wrong?" if the listener has given you a reason for their unfortunate condition.

to express sympathy for a person's negative condition using "I'm sorry to hear that" or "I hate to hear that."

to give advice pertaining to a person's condition out of concern.

when you have an ache of some sort, you can use adjectives to describe the severity of that ache. "A little headache" is a minor headache, "a headache" is a normal headache and "a terrible headache" is a severe headache.

to offer an expression of support before you conclude a conversation with someone who is not feeling well.

when a person offers you an expression of support, follow it up with an expression of gratitude.

 # SMALL TALK

Under the Weather

When a person says "I'm feeling under the weather" it means that they are not feeling good. They could be sick, sad, stressed, depressed or in another negative condition. You can also use "a little" before "under the weather" to indicate a minor negative condition or the intensifier "really" for a more severe negative condition.

> I'm feeling under the weather. (normal)
> I'm feeling a little under the weather. (minor)
> I'm feeling really under the weather.

lesson 4
Shopping for Clothes

 **INTRODUCTION**

TARGET TALK	
	Excuse me.
	I'm looking for a (pair of) **CLOTHING ITEM**.
(Do you have) any preference?	(I prefer) (a) **TYPE** + **CLOTHING ITEM**.
How about <u>this</u> / <u>these</u> **COLOR** one(s)?	(Yes, <u>that</u> / <u>those</u> look(s) good.) No, I'd rather have (a) **COLOR** one(s).
Do you have that in (a) **SIZE** (size)? Do you have those in size **#**?	Yes, (I believe) we do. Here you are! No, I'm sorry. We're out of stock.
	Thank you (very much)!
How much (<u>is it</u>) / (<u>are they</u>)?	(It's) / (They're) **PRICE**.
	That's a good deal! (I'd like to try <u>it</u> / <u>them</u> on). That's (a little) expensive.
Can I get a discount?	

* *Anything in (parentheses) is optional.*

Everyday Conversations **045**

 # BUILDING BLOCKS

EXPRESSIONS	
QUESTIONS	STATEMENTS
	Excuse me.
	I'm looking for a (pair of) **CLOTHING ITEM**.
(Do you have) any preference?	I prefer (a) **TYPE** + **CLOTHING ITEM**.
How about <u>this</u> / <u>these</u> **COLOR** one(s)?	Yes, <u>that</u> / <u>those</u> look(s) good.
	No, I'd rather have (a) color one(s).
Do you have that in (a) **SIZE** (size)?	Yes, (I believe) we do. Here you are!
Do you have those in size **#**?	No, I'm sorry. We're out of stock.
How much <u>is it</u> / <u>are they</u>?	**PRICE** dollars.
	That's a good deal!
	I'd like to try <u>it</u> / <u>them</u> on.
	That's (a little) expensive.
Can I get a discount?	

VOCABULARY						
CLOTHING ITEMS	TYPE	COLOR	SIZE		PRICE	
a jacket a sweater (a pair of) jeans (a pair of) shoes	leather (*jacket*) cardigan (*sweater*) boot-cut (*jeans*) loafers (*shoes*)	brown black white red light blue dark blue light brown dark brown	**SIZE** medium large	**#** eighty-four (84) (*jeans*) two-sixty (260) (*shoes*)	twenty (20) sixty (60) seventy (70) eighty (80)	dollars.
EXPRESSIONS			OTHERS			
Excuse me. Here you are. That's a good deal! That's (a little) expensive. Can I get a discount?			~out of stock ~in stock ~try it on ~try them on			

LESSON REVIEW

B: Excuse me. I'm looking for a (pair of) **CLOTHING ITEM**.
A: (Do you have) any preference?
B: I prefer a **TYPE** + **CLOTHING ITEM**.
A: How about <u>this</u> / <u>these</u> **COLOR** one(s)?

B1: Yes, <u>that</u> / <u>those</u> look(s) good.
Do you have <u>that</u> / <u>those</u> in (a) **SIZE** / in a **SIZE #**?

B2: I'd rather have a **COLOR** one.

A1: Yes, (I believe) we do. (Ah!) Here you are.
B: Thank you (very much). How much <u>is it</u> / <u>are they</u>?
A: **PRICE** dollars.

A2: No, I'm sorry. We're out of stock.

B1: That's a good deal! I'd like to try <u>it</u> / <u>them</u> on.   B2: That's (a little) expensive. Can I get a discount?

GRAMMAR REFRESH	
for	"for" is used in this lesson to indicate an object. *I'm looking for a jacket*.
a	"a" is used as an article in this lesson to indicate an indefinite, non-specific thing. *I'm looking for a jacket*.
this / that	"this" is used in this lesson to identify something close to the speaker. "that" is used to identify something previously mentioned observed by the speaker. A: *How about this black one*? B: *That looks good*.
these / those	"these" is used to identify a number of things close to the speaker. "those" is used to identify a number of things previously mentioned observed by the speaker. A: *How about these black ones?* B: *Those look good*.
Subject-Verb Agreement	With singular subjects be sure to add "s" at the end of the verb (That look**s**~). No "s" is needed if the subject is plural (Those look~)
one / ones ... any	"one" refers to something previously mentioned or easily identified. A: *I'm looking for a sweater*. B: *How about this black one*? "ones" is the plural form which refers to a number of things previously mentioned or easily identified. A: *I'm looking for jeans*. B: *How about these light blue ones*? When asking whether a plural or dual item of clothing is in stock you want to use "*any*" and not "ones" Thus, the question should read "Do you have *any* in stock?"
How much?	Single Items of Clothing : How much is it? Dual Items of Clothing : How much are they?
in	"in" is used in this lesson with the function of showing how things are divided. *in* large ; *in* (size) two-sixty?
try on	Single Item of Clothing (a sweater, a jacket): *I'd like to try it on*. Dual Clothing Items (jeans, shoes): *I'd like to try them on*.
I am = I'm ; That is = That's ; I would = I'd	

ROLE PLAY

DIALOGUE 1

B: Excuse me. I'm looking for a jacket.
A: (Do you have) any preference?
B: I prefer a leather jacket.
A: How about this black one?

↙ ↘

B1: Yes, that looks good.
   Do you have that in (a) medium?
A1: Yes, (I believe) we do. Here you are.

B2: I'd rather have a brown one.
A2: No, I'm sorry. We're out of stock.

B1: Thank you (very much). How much (is it)?
A1: Sixty dollars. ($60)

↙ ↘

B1: That's a good deal! (I'd like to try it on).

B2: That's (a little) expensive.
   Can I get a discount?

STRAIGHT TALK

B: **Excuse me, I'm looking for a black, leather jacket in large. Do you have one in stock?**
A: Yes, I believe we do. Here you are.

DIALOGUE 2

B: Excuse me. I'm looking for a sweater.
A: (Do you have) any preference?
B: I prefer a cardigan.
A: How about this white one?

↙ ↘

B1: Yes, that looks good.
   Do you have that in (a) large?
A1: Yes, (I believe) we do.
   Here you are.

B2: I'd rather have a red one.
A2: No, I'm sorry. We're out of stock.

B: Thank you (very much). (How much is it)?
A: Twenty dollars. ($20)

↙ ↘

B1: That's a good deal!
   I'd like to try it on.

B2: That's (a little) expensive.
   Can I get a discount?

STRAIGHT TALK

B: **Excuse me, I'm looking for a white cardigan in large. Do you have one in stock?**
A: Yes, I believe we do. Here you are.

* Anything in (parentheses) is optional.

DIALOGUE 3

B: Excuse me. I'm looking for a pair of **jeans**.
A: (Do you have) any preference?
B: I prefer **boot cut jeans**.
A: How about these **light blue** ones?

B1: Yes, those look good. Do you have those in (a) size **eighty-four**? (84)
A1: Yes, (I believe) we do. Here you are.

B2: I'd rather have **dark blue** ones.
A2: No, I'm sorry. We're out of stock.

B1: Thank you. How much (are they)?
A1: **Forty dollars**. ($40)

B1: That's a good deal! I'll take them! (I'd like to try them on).

B2: That's (a little) expensive. Can I get a discount?

STRAIGHT TALK

B: **Excuse me, I'm looking for a pair of boot-cut jeans in size eighty-four. (84) Do you have any in stock?**
A: Yes, I believe we do. Here you are.

DIALOGUE 4

B: Excuse me. I'm looking for a pair of **shoes**.
A: (Do you have) any preference?
B: I prefer **loafers**.
A: How about these **light brown** ones?

B1: Yes, those look good. Do you have those in (a) size **two-sixty**? (260)
A1: Yes, (I believe) we do. Here you are.

B2: I'd rather have **dark brown** ones.
A2: No, I'm sorry. We're out of stock.

B1: Thank you. How much (are they)?
A1: **Seventy dollar**s. ($70)

B1: That's a good deal! I'll take them! (I'd like to try them on).

B2: That's (a little) expensive. Can I get a discount?

STRAIGHT TALK

B: **Excuse me, I'm looking for a pair of light-brown loafers in size two-sixty. Do you have any in stock?**
A: Yes, I believe we do. Here you are.

Everyday Conversations

PRACTICE

DO IT YOURSELF!

Write your two dialogues of your own!

DIALOGUE 1

A:

B:

A:

B:

A:

B:

A:

B:

DIALOGUE 2

A:

B:

A:

B:

A:

B:

A:

B:

 **LISTEN AND FILL IN**

B : _____ .

A : Do you have any preference?

B : _____ .

A : How about this light blue one?

B : _____ .

A : Yes, I believe we do. Here you are.

B : _____ .

A : Fifty dollars.

B : _____ .

 **TALKING TIPS**

#1 Sizes such as "*small*", "*medium*" and "*large*" are quite universal across countries. These sizes will also be attached to such clothing items like sweaters, t-shirts and jackets. However, these simple universal sizes do not come attached to clothing items such as belts, shoes, dress shirts and others which require a measurement for an appropriate fit on a person. These numerical measurements are going to vary by country.

For instance, shoe sizes will differ between Korea and the US. If a female is looking for shoe sized "230" in Korea, the comparable size in the US will be "6." Thus, the customer can ask the store clerk, "*Do you have those (shoes) in (size)* 230 / 6?"

On the next page there is a chart (divided amongst females and males) which provides common conversions in size from the standard international sizes to sizes in Korea, the USA and Europe.

Continued on next page ➡

FEMALES: CLOTHING SIZE CONVERSION

	Extra Small	Small	Medium	Large	Extra Large
International	XS	S	M	L	XL
Korea	44	55	66	77	88
USA	0-2	4-6	8-10	12	14
Europe	32	34-36	38-40	42	44

FEMALES: MEASUREMENT

Bust	81-83cm	32in
	83-89cm	33-34in
	89-96cm	35-37in
	96-103cm	38-40in
	103-107cm	42in
Waist	61-63cm	24in
	63-68cm	25-26in
	68-75cm	27-29in
	75-81cm	30-32in
	81-86cm	34in
Hip	86-89cm	34in
	89-92cm	35-36in
	92-99cm	37-39in
	99-106cm	40-42in
	106-112cm	44in

FEMALES: SHOE SIZE CONVERSION

Korea	220	225	230	235	240	245	250	255	260
USA	5	5.5	6	6.5	7	7.5	8	8.5	9
Europe	35	36	36.5	37	37.5	38	38.5	39	40

MALES: CLOTHING SIZE CONVERSION

	Extra Small	Small	Medium	Large	Extra Large
International	XS	S	M	L	XL
Korea	90	95	100	105	110
USA	14 – 14.5	15-15.5	15.5-16	16.5-17	17.5
Europe	36-37	38-39	40-41	42	

MALES: *SHOE SIZE CONVERSION*									
Korea	240	245	250	255	260	265	270	275	280
USA	6	6.5	8	7.5	8	8.5	9	9.5	10
Europe	38	38.5	40	40	40.5	41	42	42.5	43

#2 If you want to try some clothes on, you can ask the store clerk "*Where's the fitting room*?" if you cannot find the fitting room or "*Is there a fitting room*?" if you're unsure if the clothing store has a fitting room. If you know where the fitting room is at, you can just go in there and try on your clothes!

#3 Store clerks at clothing stores will often walk by you and ask you "*Can I help you with anything*?" If you do not need any help, you can reply back with "*No, thank you. Just looking.*" If you do need help, you can begin your reply with "*Yes, I'm looking for~*" and then proceed to tell the clerk what you're looking for.

#4 Saying "*I'm looking for a sweater / a jacket / a pair of jeans / a pair of shoes*" is a fairly broad statement as there are different types and brands of sweaters, jackets, jeans and shoes. Upon hearing this statement, the store clerk may try to gain more detailed information from you concerning what you're looking for by asking you "*Do you have any preference*?" or "*Are you looking for anything in particular*?" From here, you can present more details by saying "*I prefer a cardigan / a leather jacket / a pair of boot-cut jeans / a pair of loafers.*" You can also used a more detailed description when telling the store clerk what you're looking for (*I'm looking for a pair of boot-cut jeans*.)

#5 "*Rather*" is an adverb which carries a similar meaning to "*prefer*." When given two or more choices of something, we will use "*rather*" to indicate our preference. For instance, a person can ask you the question "*Do you prefer pizza or spaghetti*?" If you prefer spaghetti you can answer with either "*I prefer spaghetti*" or "*I'd rather have spaghetti.*" We're often going to use the "*I + would*" combination with "*rather*" as it expresses a strong willingness or desire.

#6 We often use the phrase "*a pair of*" before dual sets of clothing, but it's also an optional phrase, as you can either say "*I'm looking for a pair of jeans*" or "*I'm looking for jeans.*" The only difference in meaning will be is if you use "*a pair of*" it may mean that you are looking for one set of jeans. If you do not use "*a pair of*", the meaning may convey that you are looking for more than one set of jeans.

COMMUNICATION VARIATIONS

I'm looking for	**SINGLE ITEMS OF CLOTHING** a *do not add "s" at the end of the word! (I'm looking for a jacket.) Using "a" demonstrates that you are looking to purchase a clothing item. the *add "s" at the end of the word. (I'm looking for the jackets.) Using "the" demonstrates that you are looking for the location of the clothing item.
	DUAL ITEMS OF CLOTHING a pair of some *Using "some" or "a pair of" indicates that you are wanting to purchase a clothing item. the *Using "the" indicates that you are wanting to find the location of the clothing item.
	SINGLE ITEMS OF CLOTHING a this that
	DUAL ITEMS OF CLOTHING a pair of these those

HOW MUCH?

ten	sixty	
twenty	seventy	bucks.
thirty	eighty	
forty	ninety	dollars.
fifty	<u>a</u> / <u>one</u> hundred	

JACKET	SWEATER	SHIRT	OTHERS
fleece jacket(s).	cardigan sweater(s).	camp shirt(s).	belt(s).
leather jacket(s).	pull-over sweater(s).	dress shirt(s).	hat(s).
parka(s).	sweater vest(s).	Henley shirt(s).	muffler(s).
raincoat(s).	turtle-neck sweater(s).	polo shirt(s).	tie(s).
winter coat(s).	v-neck sweater(s).	t-shirt(s).	vest(s).

JEANS	PANTS	SHOES	OTHERS
baggy jeans.	cargo pants.	boots.	boxers.
boot-cut jeans.	dress pants.	dress shoes.	pajamas.
regular jeans.	jeans.	loafers.	sunglasses.
skinny jeans.	khaki pants.	pumps.	socks.
work jeans.	slacks.	running / tennis shoes.	underwear.

Single Item of Clothing	in	→	**SIZE** extra small. small. medium. large. extra large. double x (XXL). triple x (XXXL).
Dual Item of Clothing	in (size) #. Size numbers for pants, shoes, dress shirts and more are going to vary and differ by country.		

COLORS

pink	black
purple	(dark / navy / light) blue
red	(dark / light) brown
white	(dark / light) green
yellow	maroon
	orange

Everyday Conversations **055**

 # LESSON WRAP-UP

Remember

to be mindful of the varying different sizes across countries!

to appropriately use pronouns and to-be forms with single items of clothing and dual items of clothing.

when saying "I'm looking for a jacket / a sweater / a pair of jeans / a pair of shoes", the store clerk may ask for further information regarding your preferences since jackets, sweaters, jeans and shoes come in many different types and brands. You can also use a more detailed response with your preference to the clerk so they can automatically know what you're looking for.

 # SMALL TALK

Duds

"Duds" is an informal word for "clothes." You can use the word in the pattern used in this lesson "I'm looking for some duds." In old English, a "dud" was described as a "sloppily" dressed person, but eventually the word "dud" became an informal word for clothes. "Dud" is also an informal term for something that doesn't work properly thus making it useless (*This computer's a dud.*)

lesson 5
Exchanges and Refunds

 **INTRODUCTION**

TARGET TALK	
How may I help you?	➡ I'd like to return <u>this</u> / <u>these</u> **CLOTHING ITEM** for a refund.
What seems to be the problem?	➡ <u>It's</u> / <u>They're</u> too **PROBLEM** for me.
Do you have your receipt?	➡ Yes, here you are. No, I don't (have it on me).
Would you like your refund added to your card or in cash?	➡ (I'd like it) <u>added to my card</u> / <u>in cash</u>. I'm sorry, but we cannot provide a refund without a receipt.
What are my options?	➡ We can offer you an exchange or store credit. I'll take the <u>exchange</u> / <u>store credit</u>.

✶ *Anything in (parentheses) is optional.*

 # BUILDING BLOCKS

EXPRESSIONS

QUESTIONS	STATEMENTS
How may I help you?	I'd like to return this / these **CLOTHING ITEM** for a refund.
What seems to be the problem?	It's / They're too **PROBLEM** for me.
Do you have your receipt?	Yes, here you are. No, I don't (have it on me).
Would you like your refund added to your card or in cash?	(I'd like it) added to my card / in cash. I'm sorry, but we cannot provide a refund without a receipt.
What are my options?	We can offer you an exchange or store credit. I'll take the exchange / store credit.

VOCABULARY

CLOTHING ITEM	PROBLEM	OTHERS
a raincoat	(too) big	to return
a vest	(too) small	to provide
shorts	(too) tight	to offer
slacks	(too) baggy	a receipt
		a problem
		~added to one's card
		~in cash
		an exchange
		store credit
		options

EXPRESSIONS

Here you are.
I'm sorry.

LESSON REVIEW

A: How may I help you?
B: I'd like to return <u>this</u> / <u>these</u> **CLOTHING ITEM** for a refund.
A: What seems to be the problem?
B: <u>It's</u> / <u>They're</u> too **PROBLEM** for me.
A: Do you have your receipt?

Receipt: Refund	No Receipt: Exchange or Store Credit
B: Yes, here you are. A: Would you like your refund added to your card or in cash? B: (I'd like it) <u>added to my card</u> / <u>in cash</u>.	B: No, I don't (have it on me). A: I'm sorry, but we cannot provide a refund without your receipt. B: What are my options? A: We can offer you an exchange or store credit. B: I'll take the <u>exchange</u> / <u>store credit</u>.

GRAMMAR REFRESH

a / an	"a" is used to indicate a single, indefinite object beginning with a consonant sound and "an" is used to indicate a single, indefinite object beginning with a vowel sound. *I'd like a refund. ; I'd like an exchange.*
the	"the" is used here to indicate something known, previously mentioned or definite to the speaker. A: *We can offer you an <u>exchange</u> or store credit.* B: *I'll take <u>the</u> <u>exchange</u>.*
It's / They're	It's (It is) is used when referring to a single object of clothing previously mentioned or known. *I'd like to return this <u>raincoat</u>. <u>It's</u> too big for me.* They're (They are) is used when referring to a dual item of clothing previously mentioned of known. *I'd like to return these <u>shorts</u>. <u>They're</u> too big for me.*
too	"too" is used here to indicate the "excessiveness" of the following adjective. *These shorts are <u>too</u> <u>big</u> for me.*
or	"or" is a conjunction that expresses different alternatives. *We can offer you an <u>exchange</u> or <u>store credit</u>.*
on	"on" is used in this lesson to indicate "in possession of." *I don't have my receipt <u>on</u> <u>me</u>.*
me	"me" is used by the speaker to refer to himself or herself as the object. *I don't have my receipt on <u>me</u>.*
but	"but" is used to introduce a contrasting point to something previously mentioned. *I'm sorry, <u>but</u> we cannot provide a refund.*
we	"we" is used by the speaker to refer to him or herself along with a group a people they are associated with. Typically, store clerks will use "we" to refer to the entire group of people working with in a store. *<u>We</u> (me and the people who work here) can offer you an exchange or store credit.*
cannot	"cannot" means "to not be able to." ; also: *can't* We <u>cannot</u> offer a refund.
without	"without" means "to be in absence of". *We cannot offer a refund <u>without</u> a receipt.*
	I would = I'd; It is = It's ; They are = They're; do not = don't

Everyday Conversations

 # ROLE PLAY

DIALOGUE 1

A: How may I help you?
B: I'd like to return this **raincoat** for a refund.
A: What seems to be the problem?
B: It's too **big** for me.
A: Do you have your receipt?

Receipt: Refund	No Receipt: Exchange or Store Credit
B: Yes, here you are. A: Would you like your refund added to your card or in cash? B: (I'd like it) added to my card.	B: No, I don't (have it on me). A: I'm sorry, but we cannot provide a refund without your receipt. B: What are my options? A: We can offer you an exchange or store credit. B: I'll take the exchange.

STRAIGHT TALK

A: How may I help you?
B: **I'd like to return this raincoat**, **but I don't have my receipt on me**.

DIALOGUE 2

A: How may I help you?
B: I'd like to return this **vest** for a refund.
A: What seems to be the problem?
B: It's too **small** for me.
A: Do you have your receipt?

Receipt: Refund	No Receipt: Exchange or Store Credit
B: Yes, here you are. A: Would you like your refund added to your card or in cash? B: (I'd like it) added to my card.	B: No, I don't (have it on me). A: I'm sorry, but we cannot provide a refund without your receipt. B: What are my options? A: We can offer you an exchange or store credit. B: I'll take the store credit.

STRAIGHT TALK

A: How may I help you?
B: **I'd like to return this vest**, **but I don't have my receipt on me**.

DIALOGUE 3

A: How may I help you?
B: I'd like to return these **shorts** for a refund.
A: What seems to be the problem?
B: They're too **tight** for me.
A: Do you have your receipt?

Receipt: Refund	No Receipt: Exchange or Store Credit
B: Yes, here you are. A: Would you like your refund added to your card or in cash? B: (I'd like it) in cash.	B: No, I don't (have it on me). A: I'm sorry, but we cannot provide a refund without your receipt. B: What are my options? A: We can offer you an exchange or store credit. B: I'll take the exchange.

STRAIGHT TALK

A: How may I help you?
B: **I'd like to return these shorts for an exchange**.

DIALOGUE 4

A: How may I help you?
B: I'd like to return these **slacks** for a refund.
A: What seems to be the problem?
B: They're too **baggy** for me.
A: Do you have your receipt?

Receipt: Refund	No Receipt: Exchange or Store Credit
B: Yes, here you are. A: Would you like your refund added to your card or in cash? B: (I'd like it) added to my card.	B: No, I don't (have it on me). A: I'm sorry, but we cannot provide a refund without your receipt. B: What are my options? A: We can offer you an exchange or store credit. B: I'll take the exchange.

STRAIGHT TALK

A: How may I help you?
B: **I'd like to return these slacks for store credit**.

 **PRACTICE**

DO IT YOURSELF!

Write your two dialogues of your own!

DIALOGUE 1

A:
B:
A:
B:
A:
B:
A:
B:

DIALOGUE 2

A:
B:
A:
B:
A:
B:
A:
B:

LISTEN AND FILL IN

A : How may I help you?

B : _____.

A : What seems to be the problem?

B : _____.

A : Do you have your receipt?

B : _____.

A : I'm sorry, but we cannot provide a refund without a receipt.

B : _____.

A : We can offer you an exchange or store credit.

B : _____.

TALKING TIPS

#1 Clothing stores and other department stores are all going to have different policies for issuing and exchanging refunds. In most circumstances, a receipt is needed to be issued a refund. If you do not have a receipt, it's up to the policy of the store to determine whether to grant you a refund, a store credit or an exchange. Sometimes, nothing can be done if you do not have a receipt.

#2 There's always an issue when returning an item of clothing. Typically, the clothes are too baggy, too tight, too small or too big for you. There may be other reasons as well which are listed in the Communication Variations table. Perhaps, the clothes just aren't your style or perhaps a family member gave you clothes you don't like for a birthday or Christmas gift. Whatever the reason, the store clerk processing refunds and exchanges will often ask you what the problem "*seems*" or "*appears*" to be. As long as you have your receipt, you should have no problems getting the refund. Just state your reason for returning the items!

#3 Let's say you got a shirt you like, but it's too big for you. In this case, you can go back to the store and ask to "*swap*" (to trade) the same shirt in a smaller side. You can tell the store clerk:
"*This shirt's too big for me. I'd like to swap it for a smaller size.*"
If the shirt's too small for you, you can say:
"*This shirt's too small for me. I'd like to swap it for a bigger size.*"

COMMUNICATION VARIATIONS

RETURNING ITEMS OF CLOTHING

I'd like to return
polite

I need to return
expresses necessity

I want to return
more direct

this →

SINGLE ITEMS OF CLOTHING
t-shirt(.)
dress(.)
dress shirt(.)
hat(.)
jacket(.)
muffler(.)
raincoat(.)
skirt(.)
vest(.)
watch(.)

these →

DUAL ITEMS OF CLOTHING
boxers(.)
earrings(.)
jeans(.)
pants (.)
shoes(.)
shorts(.)
slacks(.)
socks(.)
sunglasses(.)

COMMON PROBLEMS ASSOCIATED WITH RETURNED CLOTHES

This + *single item of clothing* + **is**
It's

These + *dual item of clothing* + **are**
They're

(too) →

baggy(.)
big(.)
loose(.)
small(.)
tight(.)

→ <u>for</u> / <u>on</u> me.

064 Pragmatic Talk

RETURNING ITEMS OF CLOTHING

for ➡️ an exchange.

a refund.

(a) store credit.

COMMON PROBLEMS ASSOCIATED WITH RETURNED CLOTHES

OTHER PROBLEMS

It doesn't fit. / They don't fit.
It's torn / ripped.
I don't like it / them.
It's not my style. / They're not my style.
The button / zipper is broken.

 # LESSON WRAP-UP

> **Remember**
>
> **that** clothing stores and department stores are all going to have different policies related to refunds and exchanges.
>
> **to** use pronouns and to-be verbs correctly when discussing single and dual item clothing.
>
> **that** there could be other reasons besides size-related issues for returns and you can state these reasons for your request for a refund, exchange or store credit.
>
> **that** if you like an item of clothing, but the size doesn't fit you correctly, that you can swap for the same item, given that the store has it in stock.

 # SMALL TALK

Secret Circus Jeans

Secret Circus Jeans have the distinction of being the most expensive jeans in the world with a record cost of over one million US dollars. Typically worn by females, Secret Circus Jeans have diamonds sewed into both back-pockets which give the jeans their ultra-expensive price. Try returning those jeans for refund!

lesson 6
At the Hair Salon

 **INTRODUCTION**

TARGET TALK	
What can I do for you today?	➡ I'd like my hair~ and **STYLE**, please.
So, you want # centimeters cut off the length, correct?	➡ Yes, that's correct.
Would you like anything else?	➡ I'd also like my hair <u>colored</u> / <u>dyed</u>. I'd also like to add <u>highlights</u> / <u>streaks</u> to my hair. No, that's all.
Which color?	➡ (I'd like my hair <u>colored</u> / <u>dyed</u>) **COLOR**. I'd like to add **COLOR** <u>highlights</u> / <u>streaks</u> to my hair.

* *Anything in (parentheses) is optional.*

 **BUILDING BLOCKS**

EXPRESSIONS	
QUESTIONS	STATEMENTS
What can I do for you today?	I'd like my hair~ and STYLE, please.
(So), you want # centimeters cut off the length, correct?	Yes, that's correct.
Would you like anything else?	I'd also like my hair colored / dyed.
	I'd also like to add highlights / streaks to my hair.
	No, that's all.
Which color?	(I'd like my hair colored / dyed) COLOR.
	I'd like to add COLOR highlights / streaks to my hair.

VOCABULARY				
STYLE	COLOR	# (CENTIMETERS)	OTHERS	EXPRESSIONS
permed	light brown	ten centimeters	~above / below the shoulders	That's all.
layered	golden brown	twelve centimeters	~below the ears	
straightened	blonde		~off the length	
	platinum		colored	
			dyed	
			~to add	
			highlights	
			streaks	
			split ends	
			trimmed	

LESSON REVIEW

A: What can I do for you today?
B:

I'd like my split ends	trimmed and my hair **STYLE**.		
I'd like my hair	trimmed	and **STYLE**, please.	
	cut	just <u>above</u> / <u>below</u>	the shoulders and **STYLE**, please.
		just below	the ears and **STYLE**, please.

A: Would you like anything else?

B1: I'd also like my hair <u>colored</u> / <u>dyed</u>.   B2: No, that's all.
    I'd also like to add <u>highlights</u> / <u>streaks</u> to my hair.

A: Which color?
B: (I'd like my hair <u>colored</u> / <u>dyed</u>) **COLOR**.
    I'd like to add **COLOR** <u>highlights</u> / <u>streaks</u> to my hair.

FOR CUTS OFF THE LENGTH ONLY
A: So, you want **#** centimeters cut off your length, correct?
B: Yes, that's correct.

GRAMMAR REFRESH

my	"my" is a possessive pronoun indicating something belonging to or associated with the speaker. *I'd like <u>my</u> <u>hair</u> trimmed*.
just	"just" is used in this lesson to indicate "barely" or "at the bare minimum." *I'd like my hair cut <u>just</u> <u>above the shoulders</u>*.
and	"and" is a conjunction used to combine two or more words or phrases together into a complete statement. *I'd like my hair <u>trimmed</u> <u>and</u> <u>permed</u>*.
so	"so" is used here to begin a question by referring to something previously mentioned to seek clarification. A: *<u>I'd like my hair cut just above the shoulders</u>*. B: *<u>So</u>, <u>you want about 10 centimeters cut off your length, correct</u>?*
about	"about" is used in this lesson to express "approximation." *So, you want <u>about</u> <u>10 centimeters</u> cut off your length, correct?*
that	"that" is used in this lesson to refer to something previously mentioned. A: *So, you want about 10 centimeters cut off your length, correct?* B: *Yes, <u>that</u>'s correct*.
also	"also" is used to express "in addition to." *I'd like my hair trimmed. I'd <u>also</u> like it layered*.
it	"it" refers to a thing previously mentioned, in this case "hair." "Hair" is an uncountable noun, do you'll want to use "it" when referring to "hair" after it's been previously mentioned. *I'd like my <u>hair</u> trimmed. I'd also like <u>it</u> layered*.
to	"to" is used to mark an infinitive (<u>to</u> <u>add</u>) and to indicate the thing being affected. (*I'd like to add highlights <u>to</u> <u>my hair</u>*.)
	I would = I'd ; that is = that's

Everyday Conversations

ROLE PLAY

DIALOGUE 1

A: What can I do for you today?
B: I'd like my hair cut just above the shoulders and layered, please.
A: (So), you want about ten centimeters cut off the length, correct?
B: Yes, that's correct.
A: (Would you like) anything else?

B1: Yes, I'd also like it colored.   B2: No, that's all.

A: Which color?
B: (I'd like my hair colored) light brown.

STRAIGHT TALK

A: What can I do for you today?
B: **I'd like my hair cut just above the shoulders and layered**, please.
   I'd also like it colored light brown.

DIALOGUE 2

A: What can I do for you today?
B: I'd like my hair cut just below the ears and straightened, please.
A: (So), you want about twelve centimeters cut off the length, correct?
B: Yes, that's correct.
A: (Would you) like anything else?

B1: Yes, I'd also like it dyed.   B2: No, that's all.

A: Which color?
B: (I'd like my hair dyed) blonde.

STRAIGHT TALK

A: What can I do for you today?
B: **I'd like my hair cut just below the ears and straightened**.
   I'd also like it dyed blonde.

DIALOGUE 3

A: What can I do for you today?
B: I'd like my split ends trimmed and my hair **permed**, please.
A: (Would you like) anything else?

B1: Yes, I'd also like to add highlights to my hair.

B2: No, that's all.

A: Which color?
B: I'd like to add **golden brown** highlights to my hair.

STRAIGHT TALK

A: What can I do for you today?
B: **I'd like my split ends trimmed**.
   I'd also like my hair permed and highlighted golden brown.

DIALOGUE 4

A: What can I do for you today?
B: I'd like my hair trimmed.
A: (Would you like) anything else?

B1: Yes, I'd also like to add streaks to my hair.

B2: No, that's all.

A: Which color?
B: I'd like to add **platinum** streaks to my hair.

STRAIGHT TALK

A: What can I do for you today?
B: **I'd like my hair trimmed, please**.
   I'd also like to add platinum streaks to my hair.

Everyday Conversations

 **PRACTICE**

DO IT YOURSELF!

Write your two dialogues of your own!

DIALOGUE 1

A:
B:
A:
B:
A:
B:
A:
B:

DIALOGUE 2

A:
B:
A:
B:
A:
B:
A:
B:

LISTEN AND FILL IN

A: What can I do for you?

B: _____.

A: Would you like anything else?

B: _____.

A: Which color?

B: _____.

TALKING TIPS

#1 When we go to a barber or a hair salon, we're most likely only going to want one thing done to our hair whether it's a trim, a dye or a perm.

With this being said, you can directly tell your barber "*I'd like my hair*~" and then state what you want done. For example, "*I'd like my hair trimmed.*" or "*I'd like my hair dyed (golden brown).*" or "*I'd like my hair permed.*"

Remember, when adding highlights or streaks, You'll want to use "to" plus the infinitive "add." For example, "*I'd like to add (blonde) highlights to my hair.*"

#2 Depending on where you're at, a barber or hair stylist may either be more accustomed to centimeters or inches when cutting. Be sure to familiarize yourself with measuring units of the country you're in so you're able to successfully inform your barber or stylist how much hair you want cut or trimmed. For instance 12 centimeters is approximately 4 ½ to 5 inches, so if you're wanting this amount taken off your length, you can tell your barber or stylist "*I'd like <u>5 inches</u> / <u>12 centimeters</u> cut off the length.*"

#3 Side-guards on hair-clippers should be addressed as well. Hair-Clippers usually come with nine size/side guards, with the 0 guard capable of leaving a "*shaved*" look (the shortest) and the 8-guard which keeps some length on the hair. For men having their sides trimmed, they can inform the barber "*Guard # on the sides.*"   Example: "*I'd like my hair trimmed. Four on the sides.*"

#4 You can also ask to have your hair washed and dried along with a cut or a trim. If you're getting your hair trimmed, you can tell your barber or stylist: "*I'd like my hair trimmed. I'd also like a wash and a dry.*"

COMMUNICATION VARIATIONS

HAIR CUT AND STYLE REQUESTS

I'd like my hair →	layered(.)
	permed(.)
	trimmed(.) →
	shaved off(.)
	straightened(.)
	washed and dried(.)
	cut →
	colored
	dyed →
I'd like →	(about)
	(a couple of)
	(a few) →
	to add →

＊ *Anything in (parentheses) is optional.*

(a little)	→	around the ears. on the sides. on top.		
(just) (right)	→	above / below below	→	the shoulders. the ears.
COLOR.				
# centimeters # inches	→	cut trimmed	→	off the length. off the sides. off the top.
COLOR	→	highlights streaks	→	to my hair.

 # LESSON WRAP-UP

Remember

to keep in mind that some countries will go by centimeters and others will use inches.

that there are nine "side guards" you can request especially when having hair cut on the side. The "0" guard cuts the hair closest to the skin while the 8 guard will leave more length.

that you do not have to follow the patterns presented in this lesson. If you're only needing one thing done to your hair, you can inform your barber or stylist "I'd like my hair~" and then tell them what you want done.
(I'd like my hair trimmed / dyed / permed).

when you're getting your hair colored (dyed) you can state the color in your statement (I'd like my hair colored / dyed + light brown). In addition, remember to use the to-infinitive (to add) when applying highlights or streak to your hair (I'd like to add highlights / streaks to my hair). You can also state which color before "highlight" or "streak" (I'd like to add + blonde + highlights / streaks + to my hair).

that you can also request to have your hair washed and dried by stating: "I'd (also) like a wash and a dry."

The Longest Hair in the World

The female with the longest hair in the world is Xie Qiuping from China. She has been growing her hair since the year 1973. As of today her hair measures in at 5.627 meters which is over 18 feet. Vietnam's Tran Van Hay is known in record books as the man with the longest hair in the world. His hair measured in at 6.8 meters which is over 22 feet long!

lesson 7
At the Cafe

 **INTRODUCTION**

TARGET TALK	
What would you like?	➡ (I'd like) (a / an) **COFFEE NAME**, please.
(Which) size (would you like)?	➡ (I'd like) (a / an) **SIZE**.
(Would you like it) hot or cold / iced?	➡ (I'd like it) **TEMPERATURE PREFERENCE**.
(Would you like) anything else?	➡ Yes, I'd also like a **CAFÉ SNACK**. No, (that's all). Thank you.
(Would you like it) for here or take out / to go?	➡ (I'd like it) (for) here. (I'd like it for) takeout. / (I'd like it) to go.

* Anything in (parentheses) is optional.

 # BUILDING BLOCKS

EXPRESSIONS	
QUESTIONS	STATEMENTS
What would you like?	(I'd like) (a / an) **COFFEE NAME**, please.
(Which) size (would you like)?	(I'd like) (a / an) **SIZE**.
(Would you like it) hot or cold / iced?	(I'd like it) **TEMP. PREF.**
(Would you like) anything else?	I'd also like a / an **CAFÉ SNACK**.
(Would you like it) for here or take out?	(I'd like it) (for) here. / (I'd like it for) take out.

VOCABULARY				
COFFEE NAME	SIZE	TEMP. PREF.	CAFÉ SNACK	OTHERS
Black Coffee	small	hot	bagel	please
Café Latte	medium	cold	muffin	thank you
Americano	large	iced	croissant	that's all
Cappuccino	extra large		cookie	(for) here
				(for) takeout
Café Macchiato	regular		donut	to go
Café Mocha	short		sandwich	
Vanilla Latte	tall		fruit cup	
Green Tea	grande		salad	
	venti			

LESSON REVIEW

A: What would you like?
B: (I'd like a) **COFFEE NAME**, please.
A: Which size (would you like)?
B: (I'd like <u>a</u> / <u>an</u>) **SIZE**.
A: (Would you like it) hot or iced?
B: (I'd like it) **TEMP. PREF**.
A: (Would you like) anything else?

B1: Yes, (I'd also like) <u>a</u> / <u>an</u> **CAFÉ SNACK**.   B2: No, (that's all). Thank you.

A: (Would you like it) for here or for takeout?
B: (I'd like it) (for) <u>here</u>. / (I'd like it for) <u>take out</u>.

	GRAMMAR REFRESH
a / an	"a" and "an" are articles that precede a single object. "a" will precede an object which begins with a consonant while "an" will follow an object that begins with a vowel. I'd like *a* black coffee. I'd like *an* Americano.
it	"it" is acting as a pronoun referring to a single object previously mentioned, in this case the order being made. A: *I'd like a <u>black coffee</u>, please.* B: *Would you like it hot or cold?*
or	"or" is used in this lesson to present an alternative. *Would you like it <u>hot</u> or <u>cold</u>?*
also	"also" is used to express "in addition to." A: *Anything else?* B: *Yes, I'd also like a bagel.*
and	"and" is used to join two words or phrases together in a complete statement. *I'd like <u>a black coffee</u> and <u>a croissant</u>, please.*
for	Used here to indicate a destination (here, take out). *I'd like it for <u>here</u>.*
	I would = I'd

Everyday Conversations

 # ROLE PLAY

DIALOGUE 1

A: What would you like?
B: (I'd like a) **black coffee**, please.
A: (Which) size (would you like)?
B: (I'd like a) **small**.
A: (Would you like it) hot or cold?
B: (I'd like it) **hot**.
A: (Would you like) anything else?

B1: Yes, I'd also like a **bagel**.   B2: No, (that's all). Thank you.

A: (Would you like it) for here or take out?
B: (I'd like it for) take out.

STRAIGHT TALK

A: What would you like?
B: **Small**, **hot black coffee and a bagel for takeout**, **please**.

DIALOGUE 2

A: What would you like?
B: (I'd like a) **Café Latte**, please.
A: (Which) size (would you like)?
B: (I'd like a) **medium**.
A: (Would you like it) hot or cold?
B: (I'd like it) **cold**.
A: (Would you like) anything else?

B1: Yes, I'd also like a **muffin**.   B2: No, (that's all). Thank you.

A: (Would you like it) for here or take out?
B: (I'd like it) (for) here.

STRAIGHT TALK

A: What would you like?
B: **I'd like a medium**, **cold Café Latte and a muffin for here**, **please**.

DIALOGUE 3

A: What would you like?
B: (I'd like an) Americano, please.
A: (Which) size (would you like)?
B: (I'd like a) medium.
A: (Would you like it) hot or iced?
B: (I'd like it) iced.
A: (Would you like) anything else?

B1: Yes, I'd also like a croissant.　　B2: No, (that's all). Thank you.

A: (Would you like it) for here or take out?
B: (I'd like it for) take out.

STRAIGHT TALK

A: What would you like?
B: I'd like a medium, iced Americano, please.

DIALOGUE 4

A: What would you like?
B: (I'd like a) Cappuccino, please.
A: Which size (would you like)?
B: (I'd like an) extra large.
A: (Would you like it) hot or iced?
B: (I'd like it) hot.
A: (Would you like) anything else?

B1: Yes, I'd also like a cookie.　　B2: No, (that's all). Thank you.

A: (Would you like it) for here or take out?
B: (I'd like it) (for) here.

STRAIGHT TALK

A: What would you like?
B: I'd like an extra large, hot Cappuccino for here, please.

Everyday Conversations

PRACTICE

DO IT YOURSELF!

Write your two dialogues of your own!

DIALOGUE 1

A:
B:
A:
B:
A:
B:
A:
B:

DIALOGUE 2

A:
B:
A:
B:
A:
B:
A:
B:

 # LISTEN AND FILL IN

A : What would you like?

B : _____ .

A : Which size?

B : _____ .

A : Hot or iced?

B : _____ .

A : For here or take out?

B : _____ .

TALKING TIPS

#1 Remember to use the word "*please*" after telling the barista your order. Using this word at the end of your statement makes your request polite. You don't have to use "*please*" at the end of each statement you make after you've used it in your first request, but if you're in the mood of being extra polite than you can.

#2 Using "*would like*" is a politer and softer version of "*want*." Most service related professionals are going to ask you "*What would you like*?" or "*How may I help you*?" rather than "*What do you want*?" which can come across as rather direct at times. It's also more polite to answer with "*I'd like*~" rather than "*I want*~."

#3 Be mindful that different cafes and coffee shops will have sizes that differ than the regular sizes of small, medium, and large.

#4 Know that you don't have to answer each question with a complete statement. Many times when people order coffee they usually provide a one word response often followed with "*please*." At the beginning of the communication it's advisable to answer in a complete statement (I'd like a coffee, please) as it conveys politeness, but a single word response (Coffee, please) is ok as well. This same rule applies to answering questions related to size (I'd like a medium ; Medium), temperature preference (I'd like it hot ; Hot) or preference to have your coffee at the café or out of the café (I'd like it to go ; To go).

#5 Whenever you order a bagel, you're probably going to be asked the question "*Would you like any cream cheese*?" or "*Do you want any cream cheese*?" You can answer this question with either a simple "*Yes*" or "*No*." You may then be asked "*What kind of cream cheese*?" which is asking you the flavor of the cream cheese you prefer. The most common flavors of cream cheese are "*plain*", "*onion*" or "*strawberry*" and you can answer with any of these responses. Would you like any cream cheese? Yes, (please). What kind of cream cheese? Plain.

COMMUNICATION VARIATIONS

What would you like? = What do you want?	I'd like a / an I want a / an
Which size would you like? = Which size do you want?	I'll have a / an I'll take a / an
Would you like it hot or cold / iced? = Do you want it hot or cold / iced?	I'd like it I want it I'll take it
Would you like anything else? = Do you want anything else?	I'd also like a / an I also want a / an I'll also have a / an I'll also take a / an
	I'd like a / an I want a / an I'll have a / an I'll take a / an

EXTRA

I'd like a bagel	with
I'd like a croissant	

That's all. = That's it.

COFFEE NAME **CAFÉ SNACK**	➡	please.
SIZE.		
TEMP. PREF.		(please).
COFFEE NAME. **CAFÉ SNACK**.		
COFFEE NAME **CAFÉ SNACK**	➡	too. as well.
EXTRA		
cream cheese. <u>jam</u> / <u>jelly</u>. butter.		(please).
butter.		

Everyday Conversations

 # LESSON WRAP-UP

Remember

to use the word "please" after answering the barista's initial question of "What would you like?" It's optional to use "please" in response to other questions which may be asked. If you want to be extra polite, you can do so, but it's not necessary. Just be sure to establish a polite tone at the beginning of the conversation.

that "What would you like?" is the politer form of asking "What do you want?" Many workers in customer service industries which sell drinks or food are often going to ask what you want using "What would you like?"

that coffee shops will have variances in sizes. Not all coffee shops are going to have the standard "small", "medium" and "large." Be sure to respond to appropriately to the sizes provided in the coffee shop. So, if a coffee shop sells a size called "Regular", use "I'd like a regular" or just "Regular."

when the barista asks you "Would you like anything else?" to use "also" before the verb "to like." "Also" conveys the meaning "in addition to." If you do not want anything else, you can just say "That's all" or "That's it" indicates you are finished ordering.

 # SMALL TALK

A Cup of Joe

Josephus Daniels was Secretary to the US Navy during World War I and was also known to be a very strict person. One of the things he banned on US Naval bases was alcoholic beverages. With all the alcohol banned from the Naval bases, the strongest drink left available for the sailors was coffee. As an insult to Daniels, the sailors would call their cups of coffee "a cup of Josephus Daniels". Eventually, this was shortened to "a cup of Joe". Next time you go to your coffee shop and the barista asks, "What would you like?", perhaps you can answer "I'd like a cup of Joe, please!"

SECTION 2

MY LIFE

"The beautiful thing about learning is nobody can take it away from you."

B.B. King

lesson 8
Basic Introductions

 **INTRODUCTION**

	TARGET TALK
	<u>Hi</u> / <u>Hello</u> / <u>Hey</u> **NAME B**. This is my friend **NAME C**.
(How do you do?)	➡ I'm **NAME B**. (It's) nice to meet you. (It's a) pleasure to meet you. (I'm) <u>pleased</u> / <u>happy</u> to meet you.
Where are you from?	➡ I'm from **COUNTRY** *or* **CITY**.
How do you two know each other?	➡ We're **WHO**?

* *Anything in (parentheses) is optional.*

Everyday Conversations

 # BUILDING BLOCKS

EXPRESSIONS

QUESTIONS	STATEMENTS
	Hi / Hello / Hey NAME B.
	This is my friend NAME C.
(How do you do?)	I'm NAME B.
	(It's) nice to meet you.
	(It's a) pleasure to meet you.
	(I'm) pleased / happy to meet you.
Where are you from?	I'm from COUNTRY or CITY.
How do you two know each other?	We're WHO?

VOCABULARY

WHO?	COUNTRY	CITY	EXPRESSIONS
friend	Canada	Seoul	**FORMAL GREETING**
childhood friend(s)	China	Pusan	How do you do?
roommate(s)	England	New York	**PLEASANTRIES**
			(It's) nice to meet you.
co-worker(s)	Korea	Paris	(I'm) pleased to meet you.
schoolmate(s)			(It's a) pleasure to meet you.
			(I'm) happy to meet you.

Pragmatic Talk

 # LESSON REVIEW

A: <u>Hi</u> / <u>Hello</u> / <u>Hey</u> **NAME B**. This is my friend **NAME C**.

B: <u>Hi</u> / <u>Hello</u> / <u>Hey</u> **NAME C**. (How do you do?) I'm **NAME B**.

C: **PLEASANTRY**, (**NAME B**).

B: **PLEASANTRY** too. Where are you from?

C: I'm from **COUNTRY** *or* **CITY**. Where are you from?

B: I'm from **COUNTRY** *or* **CITY**. How do you two know each other?

A: We're **WHO**?

	GRAMMAR REFRESH	
this	"this" is used in this lesson identify a nearby person. *This* is <u>my co-worker</u>.
my	"my" indicates an association with someone addressed by the speaker. *This is my <u>friend</u>.*
too	Used to express "in addition to" A: I'm from Paris. B: I'm from Paris *too*!
two	"two" is used in this lesson to refer to a group of two people. *How do you two know each other?*
from	"From" is a preposition used to describe the country or city where a person has residence. I'm *from* Seoul.
to	"to" marks the infinitive in this lesson. *To meet*

Everyday Conversations **091**

ROLE PLAY

DIALOGUE 1

A: Hi / Hello / Hey Charlie. This is my friend Tim.

B: Hi / Hello / Hey Tim. (How do you do?) I'm Charlie.

C: (It's) nice to meet you, (Charlie).

B: (It's) nice to meet you too. Where are you from?

C: I'm from Canada. Where are you from?

B: I'm from China. How do you two know each other?

A: We're childhood friends.

STRAIGHT TALK

A: Hello Charlie. This is my friend Tim from Canada.

B: Hi Tim. Nice to meet you. I'm Charlie.

DIALOGUE 2

A: Hi / Hello / Hey Jennifer. This is my friend Gina.

B: Hi / Hello / Hey Gina. (How do you do?) I'm Jennifer.

C: (I'm) pleased to meet you, (Jennifer).

B: (I'm) pleased to meet you too. Where are you from?

C: I'm from England. Where are you from?

B: I'm from Korea. How do you two know each other?

A: We're roommates.

STRAIGHT TALK

A: Hey Jennifer. This is my roommate from England, Gina.

B: Hi Gina. How do you do? I'm Jennifer. Pleased to meet you.

092 Pragmatic Talk

DIALOGUE 3

A: Hi / Hello / Hey James. This is my friend Cody.

B: Hi / Hello / Hey Cody. (How do you do?) I'm James.

C: (It's a) pleasure to meet you, (James).

B: (It's a) pleasure to meet you too. Where are you from?

C: I'm from Seoul. Where are you from?

B: I'm from Busan. How do you two know each other?

A: We're co-workers.

STRAIGHT TALK

A: Hello Brian. This is my co-worker, Cody.

B: Hi Cody. It's a pleasure to meet you. I'm James. Where are you from?

DIALOGUE 4

A: Hi / Hello / Hey Elaine. This is my friend Carol.

B: Hi / Hello / Hey Carol. (How do you do?) I'm Elaine.

C: (I'm) happy to meet you, (Elaine).

B: (I'm) happy to meet you too. Where are you from?

C: I'm from New York. Where are you from?

B: I'm from Paris. How do you two know each other?

A: We're schoolmates.

STRAIGHT TALK

A: Hey Elaine. This is my schoolmate, Carol.

B: Hello Carol. How do you do? Happy to meet you. I'm Elaine.

Everyday Conversations

PRACTICE

DO IT YOURSELF!

Write your two dialogues of your own!

DIALOGUE 1

A:
B:
A:
B:
A:
B:
A:
B:

DIALOGUE 2

A:
B:
A:
B:
A:
B:
A:
B:

LISTEN AND FILL IN

A: Hey Ray. This is my friend Bill.

B: _____.

C: Pleased to meet you, Ray.

B: _____.

C: I'm from New York. Where are you from?

B: _____.

A: We're roommates.

TALKING TIPS

#1 Most greetings are going to follow a casual flow. But, there are times when introductions are going to be set within situations which may be formal. "*How do you do*?", a variation of "*How are you doing*?" tends to be greeting used in such a formal situation. Unlike "*How are you doing*?", there isn't the necessity of issuing a reply.

#2 Basic introductions can follow a variety of patterns and are not bound strictly by the patterns in the dialogues associated with this lesson. When introduced to a person be sure to greet them by name (*Hi John*) and then introduce yourself by name. You can also add "*It's nice to meet you*" or some other pleasantry used in this lesson. If a pleasantry in used in when a person is introducing themselves to you be sure to follow it up as the first statement in your reply. View the table below for this situation.

SITUATION A	SITUATION B
A: Hi Ashley. How do you do? I'm Jacob. B: It's nice to meet you, Jacob. A: It's nice to meet you too.	A: Hi Ashley. I'm Jacob. It's nice to meet you. B: It's nice to meet you too.

#3 As mentioned previously most introductions are casual so it's best to communicate in a casual way. After being introduced to a person, it's common to ask where the person is from, what they do for a living and what their hobbies are (see in the table below for other questions which may asked and simple replies to give to those questions). Never ask anything personal such as how much money the person makes or details about their family.

OTHER BASIC INTRODUCTION QUESTIONS		
What do you do?	I'm a ➡	doctor / teacher / businessman / professor / chef / police officer / secretary / etc.
What do you like to do?	I like to ➡	read / watch movies / play video games / go mountain hiking / play the guitar / go shopping / etc.

Everyday Conversations

COMMUNICATION VARIATIONS

INTRODUCING A PERSON TO ANOTHER

This is * casual		
I'd like you to meet * More formal	➡ my ➡	
I'd like to introduce you to * Very formal		

EXTENSION ON PLEASANTRIES

(I'm) ➡	pleased glad happy delighted thrilled ➡
(It's) ➡	nice great wonderful a pleasure ➡

QUESTION	POSSIBLE ANSWERS
How do you two know each other? ➡	We're ➡
	We know each other from ➡

INTRODUCING A PERSON TO ANOTHER

(best) / (childhood) / (old) friend
co-worker
boss
colleague
boyfriend / girlfriend
roommate
mother / father
brother / sister

→ Name.

EXTENSION ON PLEASANTRIES

to meet you.
* casual

to make your acquaintance.
* formal

to meet you.

to make your acquaintance.

old / childhood friends.
co-workers.
colleagues.
roommates.
classmates.

school.
church.
work.
class.

 # LESSON WRAP-UP

> **Remember**
>
> **that** most introductions are going to be casual occurrences. Most are even casual in contexts which would be considered formal.
>
> **that** "How do you do?" is an optional greeting for someone you've been introduced to. It is mostly commonly used in a formal situation and it does not require a reply.
>
> **to** greet the person you've been introduced to by name and follow it up with your name. You can also say "It's nice to meet you" or some other pleasantry in your introduction to another person.
>
> **to** keep the conversation casual. Ask questions such as where the person is from, what he or she might do for a living or about what he or she likes. Don't ask questions related to money, status or personal details about family unless the person is comfortable providing those details.

 # SMALL TALK

Howdy!

"Howdy!" is an informal way to say "Hello" or "Hi." It is often thought of as an abbreviated form of "How do you do?" Although its origins are based in South England, it is primarily used in the southern states of the US as a casual greeting among friends. It's also the official greeting at Texas A&M University in located in College Station, Texas.

lesson 9
Tell Me About Your Family 1

 **INTRODUCTION**

TARGET TALK	
What does your <u>dad</u> / <u>mom</u> do?	➡ My <u>dad</u> / <u>mom</u> is a **JOB TITLE** (at *EPN**).
Do you have any siblings?	➡ Yes, I have~ *answers vary* No, I'm an only child.
What do you all like to do together?	➡ We like to **ACTIVITY** together.

* *EPN (Employment Place Name)*
* *Anything in (parentheses) is optional.*

 # BUILDING BLOCKS

EXPRESSIONS	
QUESTIONS	STATEMENTS
What does your dad / mom do?	My dad's / My mom's a JOB TITLE (at *EPN*).
Do you have any siblings?	Yes, I have~ *answers vary* No, I'm an only child.
What do you all like to do together?	We like to ACTIVITY together.

VOCABULARY			
FAMILY	TITLE	NUMBERS #	COMPARATIVES
dad	doctor	two	younger
mom	teacher	three	older
brother(s)	company employee	four	**ACTIVITIES**
sister(s)	homemaker		~play board games
siblings	banker		~go camping
only child	professor		~watch movies
	journalist		~travel to different places
	nurse		**EXPRESSIONS**
			Tell me about your family.

100 Pragmatic Talk

LESSON REVIEW

A: What does your dad do?
B: My dad's a **JOB TITLE** at **EPN**.
A: What does your mom do?
B: My mom's a **JOB TITLE** at **EPN**.
A: Do you have any siblings?

B1: Yes, I have ~ *answers vary* B2: No, I'm an only child.

A: What do you all like to do together?
B: We like to **ACTIVITY** together.

	GRAMMAR REFRESH
my	"my" is a possessive pronoun used in this lesson to indicate a person associated with the speaker. *My dad is a doctor.*
a, an	"a" and "an" are articles used to mark a single object. The article "a" will come before objects or adjectives beginning with a consonant sound and "an" will come before objects or adjectives beginning with a vowel sound. *I have a younger brother ; I have an older sister.*
at	"at" is a preposition used to mark a particular or specific place. *My dad's a doctor at XYZ Hospital.*
and	"and" is a conjunction used to join two words or phrases together into a statement. *I have an older brother and an older sister.*
to	"to" is used in this lesson to mark an infinitive (base form of verb). *to play / travel / go / watch etc.*
together	"together" used to show a close proximity with one other person or a group of people. *We like to play board games together.*
also	"also" is used to express "in addition to." *I have an older sister. I also have a younger sister.*
plurals	Add an "s" at the end of brother and sister in this lesson if there is more than one mentioned! *I have a brother and a sister. / I have two brothers and two sisters.*
	My dad's = My dad is ; My mom's = My mom is ; I'm = I am

Everyday Conversations

ROLE PLAY

DIALOGUE 1

A: What does your dad do?
B: My dad's a **doctor** (at Busan Hospital).
A: What does your mom do?
B: My mom's a **teacher** (at Busan Elementary School).
A: Do you have any siblings?

B1: Yes, I have an older sister and a younger brother.

B2: No, I'm an only child.

A: What do all of you like to do together?
B: We like to **play board games** together.

STRAIGHT TALK

A: Tell me about your family.
B: **My dad's a doctor at Busan Hospital and my mom is a teacher at Busan Elementary School. I also have an older sister and a younger brother.**

DIALOGUE 2

A: What does your dad do?
B: My dad's a **company employee** (at LG).
A: What does your mom do?
B: My mom's a **homemaker***.
  (*It's automatically implied that a homemaker works at home)
A: Do you have any siblings?

B1: Yes, I have two older sisters.

B2: No, I'm an only child.

A: What do all of you like to do together?
B: We like to **go camping** together.

STRAIGHT TALK

A: Tell me about your family.
B: **My dad's a company employee at LG and my mom is a homemaker. I also have two older sisters.**

DIALOGUE 3

A: What does your dad do?
B: My dad's a banker (at BK Bank).
A: What does your mom do?
B: My mom's a professor (at XYZ University).
A: Do you have any siblings?

B1: Yes, I have three younger brothers.   B2: No, I'm an only child.

A: What do all of you like to do together?
B: We like to watch movies together.

STRAIGHT TALK

A: Tell me about your family.
B: My dad's a banker at BK Bank and my mom's a professor at XYZ University. I also have three younger brothers.

DIALOGUE 4

A: What does your dad do?
B: My dad's a journalist (at QRS News).
A: What does your mom do?
B: My mom's a nurse (at ABC Hospital).
A: Do you have any siblings?

B1: Yes, I have four older sisters and two younger brothers.   B2: No, I'm an only child.

A: What do (all of) you like to do together?
B: We like to travel to different places together.

STRAIGHT TALK

A: Tell me about your family.
B: My dad's a journalist at QRS News and my mom's a nurse at ABC Hospital. I also have four older sisters and two younger brothers.

PRACTICE

DO IT YOURSELF!

Write your two dialogues of your own!

DIALOGUE 1

A:
B:
A:
B:
A:
B:
A:
B:

DIALOGUE 2

A:
B:
A:
B:
A:
B:
A:
B:

 **LISTEN AND FILL IN**

A : What does your dad do?

B : _____ .

A : What does your mom do?

B : _____ .

A : Do you have any siblings?

B : _____ .

A : What do you all of you like to do together?

B : _____ .

 **TALKING TIPS**

#1 As mentioned in Basic Introductions, try not to ask questions related to a person's family until you have gotten to know the person a bit. It's not that you cannot ask about family details in a basic introduction but you have to ensure that you've established a comfortable enough relationship through asking for basic information with the person before doing so.

#2 You can swap the word "*dad*" with "*father*" or "*old man*," but be mindful that "*old man*" is an informal title for addressing your own dad or another person's dad. You can also swap "*mom*" with "*mother*."

My **dad**'s a doctor at ABC Hospital.	My **mom**'s a doctor at ABC Hospital.
My **father**'s a professor at XYZ University.	My **mother**'s a professor at XYZ University.
My **old man**'s a journalist at XYZ News.	

Continued on next page ➡

#3 When someone asks you how many siblings you have, you should first answer with the oldest sibling and then with the younger siblings.

> I have an **older brother** and a **younger sister**.
>
> I have two **older sisters** and a **younger brother**.
>
> I have three **older sisters** and two **younger brothers**.

#4 You can swap the comparative "*older*" with "*big*" and "*younger*" with "*little*" when talking about your siblings. Using "*older*" and "*younger*" tends to be more formal, while using "*big*" and "*little*" is a bit more casual.

> I have a **big brother** and a **little sister**.
>
> I have two **big sisters** and a **little brother**.
>
> I have three **big sisters** and two **little brothers**.

#5 It may be a little more difficult if you have a variety of older and younger brothers and sisters. Let's say you have an older sister, an older brother, a younger sister and a younger brother. If you have a variety of different aged siblings you can use "*also*", "*too*" and "*as well*" to answer the question of "*Do you have any siblings*?" View the chart below for this situation.

	SITUATION
Do you have any siblings?	I have an older brother and sister. I **also** have a younger brother and sister.
	I have an older brother and sister. I have a younger brother and sister **too**.
	I have an older brother and sister. I have a younger brother and sister **as well**.
	Another Variation
	I have an older and younger brother and an older and younger sister.

#6 Now, let's say you come from an unusually large family with four older sisters, two older brothers, five younger sisters and three younger brothers. Well, how do you answer that? Look below in the table for this unusual situation.

	SITUATION
Do you have any siblings?	Yes, I have four older sisters, two older brothers, five younger sisters and three younger brothers.
	Yes, I have four older sisters and five younger sisters. I also have two older brothers and three younger brothers.

Another way to answer is to just list them out:
Do you have any siblings? Yes, four older sisters, two older brothers, five younger sisters (and) three younger brothers.

#7 There may be other activities you and your family enjoy doing together. If this is the case, then you can use the conjunction "and" to extend your sentence to make a fuller or more complete statement.

We like to	*Activity* **and** *Activity* together.
	Activity, *Activity* **and** *Activity* together.
We like to play board games and go camping together. We like to play board games, go camping and watch movies together.	

Everyday Conversations

COMMUNICATION VARIATIONS

COMMUNICATING ABOUT PARENTS

QUESTIONS

What does your →

- dad
- father
- old man*

*informal

→

- mom
- mother

→

do? →

COMMUNICATING ABOUT SIBLINGS

QUESTIONS | ANSWERS

Do you have any →
- siblings?
- brothers or sisters?
- sisters or brothers?

→

(Yes) I have →
- a / an / one
- two
- three
- four
- five

→

(No) →
- I don't have any →
- I'm an only child.

108 Pragmatic Talk

COMMUNICATING ABOUT PARENTS

ANSWERS

My dad's My father's My old man's He's	→	a company employee(.) a teacher(.) a homemaker(.) a secretary(.) a doctor(.) a dentist(.) a banker(.) a police officer(.) a lawyer(.) an engineer(.) a mechanic(.) a <u>chef</u> / <u>cook</u>(.) a public servant(.)	at *Employment Place Name*.
My mom's My mother's She's	→		

<u>older</u> / <u>big</u>　　→　　brother(s).
<u>younger</u> / <u>little</u>　　　　sister(s).

siblings.
brothers or sisters.
sisters or brothers.

Everyday Conversations

 # LESSON WRAP-UP

Remember

to ensure you've established a good enough or casual relationship with a person before asking for information about their family..

that you can swap "dad" with "father" or "old man", but keep in mind that "old man" is very informal. You can also swap "mom" with "mother."

that you can swap "older" with the adjective "big" and "younger" with the adjective "little" when talking about siblings.

when answering the question "Do you have any siblings?", it's customary to answer first with the older siblings and then introduce the younger siblings.

that there will be occasions where either you or someone else may have a variety of siblings of varying ages. In this case the easiest thing to do is just to "list them out" rather than communicating a full sentence, but it's up to you and whatever you feel comfortable with.

 # SMALL TALK

Black Sheep

A "black sheep" is a term used to regard the one family member who just doesn't "fit in." They typically do not follow family traditions and are viewed by their family as a "rebel" or a "nuisance." The roots of this word apply to sheep and how most sheep are "white", but occasionally due to genetics, a sheep will be "black" and will therefore stand out from the others.

My younger brother is the "black sheep" of the family.

lesson 10
Tell Me About Your Family 2

 **INTRODUCTION**

TARGET TALK	
What's your dad / mom like?	➡ He's / She's (**MODIFIER**) **CHARACTERISTIC**.
What does he / she like to do?	➡ He / She likes **HOBBY**.
What's your older / younger + brother / sister like?	➡ He's / She's a **STEREOTYPE**.

* *Anything in (parentheses) is optional.*

 # BUILDING BLOCKS

EXPRESSIONS	
QUESTIONS	STATEMENTS
What's your dad / mom like?	He's / She's (MODIFIER) CHARACTERISTIC.
What does he / she like to do?	He / She likes HOBBY.
What's your older / younger + brother / sister like?	He's / She's a STEREOTYPE.

VOCABULARY			
CHARACTERISTIC	HOBBY	STEREOTYPE	MODIFIERS
laid back	playing the guitar	sweetheart	really
outgoing	hanging out with his / her friends.	jock	very
bossy	ordering people around	drama queen	a little
shy	reading books	nerd	super
talkative	cooking		
thoughtful	learning new things		
creative	painting		
intelligent			

LESSON REVIEW

A: What's your dad like?

B: He's (MODIFIER) CHARACTERISTIC.

A: What does he like to do?

B: He likes HOBBY.

A: What's your mom like?

B: She's (MODIFIER) CHARACTERISTIC.

A: What does she like to do?

B: She likes HOBBY.

A: What's your older / younger + brother / sister like?

B: He's / She's a STEREOTYPE.

GRAMMAR REFRESH	
his / her	"his" and "her" are both possessive pronouns. "His" refers to something belonging to or associated with a male person while "her" refers to something belonging to or associated with a female person. *He's hanging out with his friends. / She's hanging out with her friends.*
Subject Verb Agreement	Singular third person pronouns such as "he" and "she" will be followed with a verb ending in "s." He likes~
modifiers	We can use the modifiers "*very*", "*really*" and "*super*" with positive, neutral and negative characteristics. He's *really* laid back. ; She's *very* shy. ; He's *super* bossy. We'll use "*a little*" with neutral or negative characteristics. She's *a little* shy. ; He's *a little* bossy.
What's someone like? vs. What does someone like to do?	When you ask "*What's someone like*?", you're asking about their characteristics. When you ask "*What's someone like to do*?", you're asking about what activities that person finds enjoyment in doing.
What's = What is; He's = He is ; She's = She is	

Everyday Conversations

ROLE PLAY

DIALOGUE 1

A: What's your dad like?
B: He's (really) **laid back**.
A: What does he like to do?
B: He likes **playing the guitar**.
A: What's your mom like?
B: She's (really) **outgoing**.
A: What does she like to do?
B: She likes **hanging out with her friends**.
A: What's your older sister like?
B: She's a **sweetheart**.

STRAIGHT TALK

A: Tell me about your family.
B: **My dad's laid back. He likes playing the guitar. My mom is really outgoing. She likes hanging out with her friends. (And) my older sister is a sweetheart.**

DIALOGUE 2

A: What's your dad like?
B: He's (very) **bossy**.
A: What does he like to do?
B: He likes **ordering people around**.
A: What's your mom like?
B: She's (a little) **shy**.
A: What does she like to do?
B: She likes **reading books**.
A: What's your older brother like?
B: He's a **jock**.

STRAIGHT TALK

A: Tell me about your family.
B: **My dad is very bossy. He likes ordering people around. My mom is a little shy. She likes reading books. (And) my older brother's a jock.**

DIALOGUE 3

A: What's your dad like?
B: He's (super) talkative.
A: What does he like to do?
B: He likes hanging out with his friends.
A: What's your mom like?
B: She's (very) thoughtful.
A: What does she like to do?
B: She likes cooking.
A: What's your younger sister like?
B: She's a drama queen.

STRAIGHT TALK

A: Tell me about your family.
B: My dad's super talkative. He likes to hang out with his friends. My mom is very thoughtful. She likes cooking. (And) my younger is sister's a drama queen.

DIALOGUE 4

A: What's your dad like?
B: He's (really) creative.
A: What does he like to do?
B: He likes painting.
A: What's your mom like?
B: She's (very) intelligent.
A: What does she like to do?
B: She likes learning new things.
A: What's your younger brother like?
B: He's a nerd.

STRAIGHT TALK

A: Tell me about your family.
B: My dad's really creative. He likes painting. My mom's very intelligent. She likes learning new things. (And) my younger brother is a nerd.

 **PRACTICE**

DO IT YOURSELF!

Write your two dialogues of your own!

DIALOGUE 1

A:
B:
A:
B:
A:
B:
A:
B:

DIALOGUE 2

A:
B:
A:
B:
A:
B:
A:
B:

 **LISTEN AND FILL IN**

A : What's your dad like?

B : ....

A : What does he like to do?

B : ....

A : What's your mom like?

B : ....

A : What does she like to do?

B : ....

A : What's your younger sister like?

B : ....

 **TALKING TIPS**

#1 Of course your family is going to have more than one characteristic, so you don't have to stick with describing family members with a single characteristic. You can add further description of your family members by using the conjunction "*and*" and "*but*".

"*And*" is going to be used to join two or more words or phrases together into a complete statement, while "*but*" is used to make a point which contrasts with prior given information.

"*And*" will keep the description of a family member consistent. For instance, if you say "My mom's laid back and friendly" the expressions "*laid back*" and "*friendly*" are both consistent in their positive connotation.

If you say your mom is "*bossy*" (which is considered a negative characteristic) you can use "*but*" to make a contrasting point and then use a positive characteristic like "*friendly*."

Continued on next page ➡

Everyday Conversations

Look below at the table for examples on how you can use "*and*" and "*but*" to describe family members.

AND	BUT
My mom is laid back and kind.	My mom is laid back, but old-fashioned.
My older brother is bossy, demanding and obnoxious.	My older sister is bossy, but thoughtful.
My dad's outgoing and hilarious.	My dad's obnoxious, but kind.

#2 Typically strong modifiers (intensifiers) like "*really*", "*very*" and "*super*" can go with positive, neutral and negative characteristics. Modifiers such as "*a little*", "*a tad*" and "*a bit*" are more appropriate with neutral and negative characteristics. Look at the table below to see how these are used in context.

MODIFIERS	
My mom is very laid back (and kind).	My mom is really laid back, but a little old-fashioned.
My older brother is really bossy (demanding and obnoxious).	My older sister is a tad bossy, but very thoughtful.
My dad's super outgoing (and hilarious).	My dad's a bit obnoxious, but really kind.

#3 You can also use "*and*" when answering about what your family members like to do. It's evident that family members will like to do more than one thing. Perhaps your dad is a creative person who likes to play guitar and paint. In that case you can answer "*What does he like to do*?" with "*He likes playing the guitar and painting*."

USING "AND" TO DESCRIBE WHAT AN INDIVIDUAL LIKES TO DO	
What does he / she like to do?	He / She likes painting and reading books.
	He / She likes painting, reading books and cooking.
	He / She likes painting, reading books, cooking and learning new things.

118 Pragmatic Talk

#4 Stereotypes are simplified ideas we assign to a person or a group of people. When describing family, especially siblings, we often use stereotypes to describe a person in our family mostly in a playful, jovial way. Usually, when someone refers to a sibling using a stereotype such as "*jock*" or "*drama queen*", they're typically joking around.

Some other stereotypes to describe an individual's characteristic are listed below in the table.

OTHER STEREOTYPES TO DESCRIBE AN INDIVIDUAL'S PERSONALITY	
	Positive Characteristics
	a ball of sunshine. *a happy person*
	a chill cat. *usually used to describe laid back males*
	an old soul *a quiet, introspective individual who is often considered to be wise beyond their age. Often used with younger people who do not share the same interests as others their own age. This can be a positive or neutral description depending on the context in which it's used.*
	Neutral Characteristics
My dad's	a muscle-head. *usually used to describe muscular males who work out a lot.*
My mom's	
My brother's	a gym-rat. *someone who exercises a lot and maintains a strict diet.*
My sister's	
	a health-nut *someone who is very serious about their health.*
	Negative Characteristics
	a goody two shoes / goody-goody. *a person who is smug and annoyingly virtuous*
	a negative ninny. *a person who is consistently pessimistic.*
	a couch potato. *a lazy person.*

COMMUNICATION VARIATIONS

DESCRIBING A PERSON'S CHARACTERISTICS

He's / She's ➡️

POSITIVE CHARACTERISTICS

outgoing.
laid back / chill.
cool.
kind.
fun.
funny / hilarious.
athletic.
creative / artistic.
intelligent / smart.
friendly.
sweet.
gentle.

ADDING MODIFIERS

He's / She's ➡️

really
very
super ➡️

a little
a tad
a bit ➡️

USING STEREOTYPES TO DESCRIBE A PERSON

He's a / an
She's a / an ➡️

POSITIVE CONNOTATION

sweetheart.
doll.
gentleman.
* for males only

lady.
* for females only

hard worker.

120 Pragmatic Talk

DESCRIBING A PERSON'S CHARACTERISTICS

NEUTRAL CHARACTERISTICS

shy / reserved.
quiet.
serious.
sensitive
talkative.
old fashioned.

NEGATIVE CHARACTERISTICS

bossy.
demanding.
loud.
obnoxious.
harsh.
insensitive.
rigid.
stupid / dumb.
dull.
gloomy.
abrasive.
boring.

ADDING MODIFIERS

Positive characteristic.
Neutral characteristic.
Negative characteristic.

Neutral characteristic.
Negative characteristic.

USING STEREOTYPES TO DESCRIBE A PERSON

NEUTRAL CONNOTATION

jock.
*typically used with athletic males

nerd.
clown.
dork.
goofball.

NEGATIVE CONNOTATION

drama queen.
weirdo.
idiot.
freeloader.
blabbermouth.
busy-body.
know-it-all.

 # LESSON WRAP-UP

Remember

that you do not need to use only one descriptive word to describe your family members. If you want to extend your answer you can use the conjunctions "and" and "but" in your answer to give a fuller answer.

use modifiers to describe to which degree of the characteristic someone in your family has. There's a difference between saying your mother is "a little shy" and "really shy." Remember that intensifiers such as "very", "really" and "super" can come before positive, neutral and negative characteristics and "a tad", "a little" and "a bit" should come before neutral and negative characteristics.

that you can answer "What does he / she like to do?" more completely by using the conjunction "and."

using stereotypes to describe siblings or other family members is a casual way to describe someone you know without providing a lot of information.

 # SMALL TALK

It Runs In the Family

"It runs in the family" is an expression used to describe a certain characteristic that is associated with the family. If members of your family are all athletes or enjoy sports you could say "Being <u>an athlete</u> / <u>a jock</u> runs in the family." This expression also extends to illnesses or ailments that may be associated with your family as well. For instance, bad backs, bad knees or weak teeth are common ailments in associated with families. You could say "<u>Bad backs</u> / <u>Bad knees</u> / <u>Weak teeth</u> run in the family."

lesson 11
Tell Me About Your Best Friend

 **INTRODUCTION**

TARGET TALK	
Do you have a best friend?	➡ Yes, <u>his</u> / <u>her</u> name's **NAME**. No, most of my friends are **TYPE OF FRIEND**.
How long have you (two) known each other?	➡ (I've known **NAME**) <u>since</u> **ERA** / <u>about</u> **#** years.
What's <u>he</u> / <u>she</u> like?	➡ He's / She's a **STEREOTYPE**. He's / She's always **DETAIL**.
What do you have in common?	➡ We both enjoy **COMMONALITY**.

* Anything in (parentheses) is optional.

Everyday Conversations

 # BUILDING BLOCKS

EXPRESSIONS

QUESTIONS	STATEMENTS
Do you have a best friend?	Yes, his / her name's NAME. No, most of my friends are TYPE OF FRIEND.
How long have you (two) known each other?	(I've known NAME) since ERA / about # years.
What's he / she like?	He's / She's a STEREOTYPE. He's / She's always DETAIL.
What do you have in common?	We both enjoy COMMONALITY.

VOCABULARY

TYPE OF FRIEND	ERA	STEREOTYPES(more)	DETAILS	COMMONALITY
best friend	childhood	straight-shooter	honest	~talking politics
acquaintance	college	funny guy	~cracking jokes	~watching movies
fair weather friends		party girl	~having fun	~going to the clubs
co-workers		intelligent guy	~learning new things	~visiting museums

# (NUMBERS)		OTHERS	
five		enjoy	
ten		years	

EXPRESSIONS

Tell me about your best friend.

 # LESSON REVIEW

A: Do you have a best friend?

B1: Yes, his / her name's NAME.   B2: No, most of my friends are TYPE OF FRIEND.

A: How long have you (two) known each other?
B: (I've known NAME) since ERA / about # years.
A: What's he / she like?
B: He's / She's a STEREOTYPE. He's / She's always DETAIL.
A: What do you have in common?
B: We both enjoy COMMONALITY.

	GRAMMAR REFRESH
her / his	"her" and "his" are both possessive pronouns. In this lesson "her" refers to something belonging to a female and "his" refers to something belonging to a male. Her name is~ / His name is~
most	"most" is used here to express the meaning of "to the greatest extent." Most of my friends are acquaintances.
of	"of" is used here to express association with a larger group. Most of my friends are acquaintances.
my	"my" is a possessive pronoun indicating something belonging to or someone associated with the speaker. my friends~
are	"are" is the plural form of "to be." Most of my friends are~
known	"known" is the past participle form of "to know" which indicates that person has been aware of someone else from an undefined point in the past to the present. I've known Ted about five years.
since	"since" is used to refer to an intervening past period of time up to the present time. I've known Ted since childhood.
always	"always" is used to express something done at all times. She's always cracking jokes.
both	"Both" is used to refer to two people in this lesson. We both like watching movies.
who	"who" is used here to introduce a clause referring to a person who was previously mentioned. Jim is an intelligent guy who enjoys visiting museums.
	name's = name is ; What's = What is ; He's / She's = He is / She is ; I've = I have

ROLE PLAY

DIALOGUE 1

A: Do you have a best friend?

B1: Yes, her name's **Anna**.   B2: No, most of my friends are **acquaintances**.

A: How long have you (two) known each other?
B: (I've known **Anna**) since **college**.
A: What's she like?
B: She's a **straight shooter**. She's always **honest**.
A: What do you (two) have in common?
B: We both enjoy **talking politics**.

STRAIGHT TALK

A: Tell me about your best friend.
B: **Her name's Anna**. **Anna's a straight shooter who's always honest**. **I've known her since college**. **We both enjoy talking politics**.

DIALOGUE 2

A: Do you have a best friend?

B1: Yes, his name's **Tommy**.   B2: No, most of my friends are **fair weather friends**.

A: How long have you (two) known each other?
B: (I've known **Tommy**) since **childhood**.
A: What's he like?
B: He's a **funny guy**. He's always **cracking jokes**.
A: What do you (two) have in common?
B: We both enjoy **watching movies**.

STRAIGHT TALK

A: Tell me about your best friend.
B: **His name's Tommy**. **He's a funny guy who's always cracking jokes**. **I've known him since childhood**. **We both enjoy watching movies**.

DIALOGUE 3

A: Do you have a best friend?

B1: Yes, her name's Leah.   B2: No, most of my friends are co-workers.

A: How long have you (two) known each other?
B: (I've known Leah) about five years.
A: What's she like?
B: She's a party girl. She's always having fun.
A: What do you (two) have in common?
B: We both enjoy going to the clubs.

STRAIGHT TALK

A: Tell me about your best friend.
B: Her name's Leah. She's a party girl who's always having fun. I've known her about five years. We both enjoy going to the clubs.

DIALOGUE 4

A: Do you have a best friend?

B1: Yes, his name's Bryan.   B2: No, most of my friends are acquaintances.

A: How long have you (two) known each other?
B: (I've known Bryan) about ten years.
A: What's he like?
B: He's an intelligent guy. He's always learning new things.
A: What do you (two) have in common?
B: We both enjoy visiting museums.

STRAIGHT TALK

A: Tell me about your best friend.
B: His name's Brian and he's an intelligent guy who's always learning new things. We both enjoy visiting museums.

PRACTICE

DO IT YOURSELF!

Write your two dialogues of your own!

DIALOGUE 1

A:
B:
A:
B:
A:
B:
A:
B:

DIALOGUE 2

A:
B:
A:
B:
A:
B:
A:
B:

 **LISTEN AND FILL IN**

A : Do you have a best friend?

B : ....

A : How long have you known each other?

B : ....

A : What's she like?

B : ....

A : What do you have in common?

B : ....

 **TALKING TIPS**

#1 Sometimes you may have one best friend or you may have several. Look at the table below for some further variances in asking and answering about best friends.

SITUATION: MORE THAN ONE BEST FRIEND	
Questions	**Possible Answers**
Do you have a best friend? Do you have any best friends?	Yes, my best friend is NAME. Yes, his / her name is NAME. Yes, my best friends are NAME and NAME. Yes, their names are NAME and NAME. Yes, my best friends are NAME, NAME and NAME. Yes, their names are NAME, NAME and NAME.
Who is your best friend? Who are your best friends?	My best friend is NAME. My best friends are NAME and NAME. My best friends are NAME, NAME and NAME.

Continued on next page ➡

#2 You will have to modify some of the stereotypes in this lesson according to gender. View the table below to see how these are adjusted by gender.

MALES	FEMALES
intelligent guy / man / boy*	intelligent lady / woman / girl**
funny guy / man / boy*	funny lady / woman / girl**
party animal***	party girl****
*"boy" indicates a young male. **girl indicates a young female ***party animal is typically associated with males, but it can also be applied to females ****although the noun "girl" is associated with a young female, the word "party girl" can be applied to a woman of any age who enjoys "partying."	

#3 Most people are going to have a small circle of best friends, but they'll also have a lot of other friends who are not considered "*best friends*." Usually when describing these "*other friends*", most people will commonly describe them as "*acquaintances*" or "*co-workers*."

#4 Friends will have many things in common. One way to express that you have more than one or two things in common is to say "*We have a lot in common*" then proceed to list talk about the things you have in common. View the table below for further variations on how to answer "*What do you have in common?*"

EXPRESSING MULTIPLE COMMONALITIES		
(We have a lot in common).	We both enjoy / like / love	*commonality* and *commonality*.
		commonality, *commonality* and *commonality*.
		commonality, *commonality*, *commonality* and *commonality*.
EXAMPLES		
(We have a lot in common).		We both enjoy talking politics and watching movies.
		We both like talking politics, watching movies and visiting museums.
		We both love talking politics, watching movies, visiting museums and going to the clubs.

#5 Keep in mind that you can also go back to Tell Me About Your Family 2 and use some of the characteristics and common stereotypes to describe what your best or other friends are like!
Look at the table below to see other ways you can incorporate these words into conversation whether you are describing a "*best*" friend, a friend in general or some other type of friend.

USING "STEREOTYPES" TO DESCRIBE A BEST FRIEND OR OTHER FRIENDS AND ACQUAINTANCES	
My best friend's My friend's My co-worker's My boss's My classmate's Name's	**Positive Connotation** an old soul. a sweetheart. **Neutral Connotation** a jock. a nerd. **Negative Connotation** a drama queen. a goody-two-shoes.
EXAMPLES	

My best friend's an old soul.

My co-worker's a goody-two-shoes.

John's a nerd.

COMMUNICATION VARIATIONS

INTRODUCING A FRIEND'S NAME		OTHER TYPES OF FRIENDS WHO AREN'T YOUR "BEST FRIEND"	
<u>His</u> / <u>Her</u> name's →	Name.	Most of my friends are →	
My best friend's name is →		Most of my other friends are →	

ANSWERING "HOW LONG HAVE YOU KNOWN EACH OTHER?"

I've known Name → I've known <u>him</u> / <u>her</u>	since →	**ERA** childhood. college. pre-school. elementary school. middle school. high school.	
	about * *approx.* for * *definite* →	**NUMBER** <u>a</u> / <u>one</u> two three four five six seven eight nine ten →	

EXPRESSING COMMONALITIES

We both <u>enjoy</u> / <u>like</u> / <u>love</u> →	**ACTIVITIES** talking politics. watching movies. visiting museums. visiting different places. shopping. having fun. cracking jokes. travelling to different countries. reading books. mountain hiking. going to the coffee shop.

acquaintances.
fair weather friends.
co-workers.
colleagues.
users.
freeloaders.
drinking buddies.
school friends.

YEAR

2010 (twenty-ten ; two thousand ten).
2001 (two thousand one).
2000 (two thousand).
1990 (nineteen ninety).
1991 (nineteen ninety one).
1980 (nineteen eighty).
1981 (nineteen eighty one).

MONTH

January.
February.
March.
April.
May.
June.
July.
August.
September.
October.
November.
December.

TIME

year(s).

month(s).

day(s).

OTHERS

spicy food.
sweets.
sports.
arts and crafts.
movies.
coffee.
museums.
Math.
English.
animals.
TV dramas.

 # LESSON WRAP-UP

Remember

that you can adjust the conversation about "a best friend" to two or more "best friends."

that you can borrow some of the characteristics and common stereotypes from Tell Me About Your Family 2 to describe a best friend or other types of friends.

to modify according to gender with "intelligent guy" and "funny guy" as "guy" is an informal noun for "man." So, you'll want to substitute that for a female noun like "lady" or "woman."

that friends who are not considered "best friends" are commonly referred to as "acquaintances" or "co-workers."

that you can express the multiple commonalities you have with friends rather than focusing on a single commonality.

 # SMALL TALK

Different Ways to Say Best Friend

There's a couple of expressions you can use to refer to a best male friend or female friend. Calling someone a "brother" or "sister" when they are not related to you by family is a way to refer to a close friend. Thus, for a best male friend you can use the expression "My brother from another mother" and for a best female friend you can use the expression "My sister from another mister."

He's my best friend. = He's my brother from another mother.
She's my best friend = She's my sister from another mister.

lesson 12
Talking About Hobbies

 **INTRODUCTION**

	TARGET TALK
Do you have any hobbies?	➡ Yes, I have plenty of hobbies. 　Tell me about them. 　My main hobby is **N-HOBBY**. 　I enjoy **N-HOBBY** too. No, I don't (have time for hobbies).
How often do you **V-HOBBY**?	➡ (I + **V-HOBBY**) + **FREQUENCY**. I'd like to **V-HOBBY** with you some time. Sure, I'd like that.
(Do you have) any other hobbies?	➡ Of course. I enjoy **N-HOBBY** and **N-HOBBY**.

* Anything in (parentheses) is optional.

BUILDING BLOCKS

EXPRESSIONS	
QUESTIONS	STATEMENTS

Do you have any hobbies?	Yes, I have plenty of hobbies.
	     Tell me about them.
	     My main hobby is N-HOBBY.
	     I enjoy N-HOBBY too.
	 No, I don't (have time for hobbies).

How often do you V-HOBBY?	(I + V-HOBBY) + FREQUENCY. I'd like to V-HOBBY with you some time. Sure, I'd like that.
(Do you have) any other hobbies?	Of course. I enjoy N-HOBBY and N-HOBBY.

VOCABULARY				
HOBBIES		FREQUENCY	EXPRESSIONS	OTHERS
Hobbies as a Noun N-HOBBY(gerund)	Hobbies as a Verb V-HOBBY	~everyday	of course	main
gardening	~(to) garden	~every weekend		hobby
rock climbing	~(to) go rock climbing	~whenever I have free time		hobbies
playing video games	~(to) play video games	~whenever I have a chance		
mountain hiking	~(to) go mountain hiking			
travelling				
cooking				
camping				
sailing				
surfing the net				
watching TV				
painting				
playing piano				

 # LESSON REVIEW

A: Do you have any hobbies?

B1: Yes, I have plenty of hobbies.   B2: No, I don't (have time for hobbies).

A: Tell me about them.
B: My main hobby is **N-HOBBY**.
A: I enjoy **N-HOBBY** too. How often do you **V-HOBBY**?
B: (I **V-HOBBY**) **FREQUENCY**.
A: I'd like to **V-HOBBY** with you some time.
B: Sure, I'd like that.
A: (Do you have) any other hobbies?
B: Of course. I enjoy **N-HOBBY** and **N-HOBBY** too.

	GRAMMAR REFRESH
plenty of~	"plenty" means a great number or quantity, more than enough, while "of" is used to show possession. *I have plenty of hobbies.*
for	"for" is used to indicate an object in this lesson. *I don't have time for hobbies.*
about	"about" is used in this lesson to express "on the subject of~" *Tell me about your hobbies.*
them	"them" is an objective pronoun which refer to two or more things previously mentioned or easily identified. A: *I have plenty of hobbies.* B: *Tell me about them.*
too	"too" is used to express "in addition to." *I like mountain hiking. I like painting too.*
to	"to" marks the infinitive in this lesson. *to go / garden / play* etc.
with	"With" is used to express accompaniment. *I'd like to garden with you.*
that	"that" refers to something previously mentioned. A: *I'd like to garden with you some time.* B: *Sure, I'd like that.*
and	"and" is used to join two or more words or phrases together into a complete statement. *I like to garden and go mountain hiking.*
	I would = I'd ; do not = don't

 # ROLE PLAY

DIALOGUE 1

A: Do you have any hobbies?

B1: Yes, I have plenty of hobbies.   B2: No, I don't have time for hobbies.

A: Tell me about them.
B: My main hobby is **gardening**.
A: I enjoy **gardening** too. How often do you **garden**?
B: (I **garden**) **every day**.
A: I'd like to **garden** with you some time.
B: Sure, I'd like that.
A: (Do you have) any other hobbies?
B: Of course. I enjoy **travelling** and **cooking** too.

STRAIGHT TALK

A: Tell me about your hobbies.
B: **My main hobby is gardening. I enjoy travelling and cooking too.**

DIALOGUE 2

A: Do you have any hobbies?

B1: Yes, I have plenty of hobbies.   B2: No, I don't have time for hobbies.

A: Tell me about them.
B: My main hobby is **rock climbing**.
A: I enjoy **rock climbing** too. How often do you **go rock climbing**?
B: (I **go rock climbing**) **every weekend**.
A: I'd like to **go rock climbing** with you some time.
B: Sure, I'd like that.
A: (Do you have) any other hobbies?
B: Of course. I enjoy **camping** and **sailing** too.

STRAIGHT TALK

A: Tell me about your hobbies.
B: **I go rock climbing every weekend. I enjoy camping and sailing too.**

DIALOGUE 3

A: Do you have any hobbies?

B1: Yes, I have plenty of hobbies.　　B2: No, I don't have time for hobbies.

    A: Tell me about them.
    B: My main hobby is playing video games.
    A: I enjoy playing video games too. How often do you play video games?
    B: (I play computer games) whenever I have free time.
    A: I'd like to play computer games with you some time.
    A: (Do you have) any other hobbies?
    B: Of course. I enjoy surfing the net and watching TV too.

STRAIGHT TALK

A: Tell me about your hobbies.
B: My main hobby is playing computer games. I enjoy surfing the net and watching TV too.

DIALOGUE 4

A: Do you have any hobbies?

B1: Yes, I have plenty of hobbies.　　B2: No, I don't have time for hobbies.

    A: Tell me about them.
    B: My main hobby is mountain hiking.
    A: I enjoy mountain hiking too. How often do you go mountain hiking?
    B: (I go mountain hiking) whenever I have a chance.
    A: I'd like to go mountain hiking with you some time.
    B: Sure, I'd like that.
    A: (Do you have) any other hobbies?
    B: Of course. I enjoy painting and playing piano too.

STRAIGHT TALK

A: Tell me about your hobbies.
B: I enjoy mountain hiking. I enjoy painting and playing piano too.

 **PRACTICE**

DO IT YOURSELF!

Write your two dialogues of your own!

DIALOGUE 1

A:
B:
A:
B:
A:
B:
A:
B:

DIALOGUE 2

A:
B:
A:
B:
A:
B:
A:
B:

 **LISTEN AND FILL IN**

A : Do you have any hobbies?

B : _____ .

A : Tell me about them.

B : _____ .

A : I enjoy rock climbing too. How often do you go rock climbing?

B : _____ .

A : I'd like to go rock climbing with you some time.

B : _____ .

A : Do you have any other hobbies?

B : _____ .

 **TALKING TIPS**

#1 You're going to have several hobbies. We all do, of course. Using the word "*main*" before the word "*hobby*" lets the listener know that this is your favorite hobby. If someone asks you "*Do you have any hobbies*?" or "*What are your hobbies*?" you can answer with "*My main hobby is*~" and then state the name of your favorite hobby.

If you have more than one main hobby, you can also extend your sentence using "and" to indicate that you have more than one hobby. You can utilize the table below for different sentence patterns you can use when referring to two or more "*main*" hobbies.

You can also answer the questions of "*Do you have any hobbies*?" or "*What are your hobbies*?" with "*I like*~" or "*I enjoy*" and then state the activity.

Continued on next page ➡

Everyday Conversations

MAIN HOBBY EXTENSION	
Do you have any hobbies? What are your hobbies?	My main hobby is **N-HOBBY**. My main hobbies are **N-HOBBY** and **N-HOBBY**. I like **N-HOBBY**. I like **N-HOBBY** and **N-HOBBY**. I enjoy **N-HOBBY**. I enjoy **N-HOBBY** and **N-HOBBY**.

#2 Gerunds are an English expression that can function both as a noun and a verb. Typically these expressions end with –ing. For example "*rock climbing*" would be considered a noun. To turn it into a verb, you would need to add "*to*" and the infinitive "*go.*" So, saying "*I like rock climbing*" means that you enjoy the activity while saying "*I like to go rock climbing*" means you like to engage in the physical action-based activity. Either way you state the expression, the listener will comprehend that you enjoy rock climbing.

Look at the table below for brief examples of how a gerund (an activity) acts as the object of a sentence. These sentences are then written in to-infinitive form in the adjoining column.

GERUND -ING FORM (ACTS AS A NOUN INDICATING AN ACTIVITY)	TO-INFINITIVE ACTS A VERB
I like **surfing the net**.	I like **to surf the net**.
I like **exercising**.	I like **to exercise**.
I like **mountain hiking**.	I like **to go mountain hiking**.
I like **swimming**.	I like **to go swimming**.
I like **walking**.	I like **to walk**.

#3 "*Like*" and "*enjoy*" share a similar meaning which means to take pleasure in doing something. However, "*like*" can be followed by a "*to-infinitive*" or an "*–ing form*" (I like to surf the net ; I like surfing the net) while "*enjoy*" cannot. "*Enjoy*" is usually going to take an object, or in this case, an –ing form (a gerund). Hence you can say "*I enjoy surfing the net*", but you CANNOT say "*I enjoy to surf the net.*" Be sure to remember this rule!

I LIKE	I ENJOY
I like mountain hiking. **I like** to go mountain hiking.	**I enjoy** mountain hiking.
I like surfing the net. **I like** to surf the net.	**I enjoy** surfing the net.
I like gardening. **I like** to garden.	**I enjoy** gardening.

#4 When answering a person's questions which ask about your hobbies you can simply answer with "*I like*~" or "*I enjoy*~" and then state the activity or activities. But, when answering in this pattern try not to use any frequencies at the end of your sentence. If you answer with "*I like to*" you transform the hobby into a verb, an action, and then it is more appropriate to place the frequency of the action at the end of the sentence (the verb "*enjoy*" does not take a to-infinitive). View the table below for examples.

AS ACTIVITIES (NO FREQUENCIES)	AS ACTIONS WITH FREQUENCIES
I like mountain hiking.	I like to go mountain hiking on the weekend.
I like painting and playing the guitar.	I like to paint and play the guitar whenever I have free time.
I like playing video games, surfing the net and reading.	I like to play video games, surf the net and read every chance I get.

COMMUNICATION VARIATIONS

DESCRIBING YOUR HOBBIES AS ACTIVITIES

I enjoy →	camping. cooking. gardening. mountain hiking. painting. playing the <u>piano</u> / <u>guitar</u>. playing video games. reading.
I like **My (main) hobby is** →	rock climbing. sailing. surfing the net. travelling. *If you want to list more than one hobby, you can use extend your sentence using the conjunction "and." EX. I <u>enjoy</u> / <u>like</u> cooking, sailing <u>and</u> surfing the net. ; My hobbies are cooking, sailing <u>and</u> surfing the net.

TALKING ABOUT HOBBIES AS ACTIONS AND INCORPORATING FREQUENCY

I like to **I** →	go camping(.) cook(.) garden(.) go mountain hiking(.) paint(.) play the <u>piano</u> / <u>guitar</u>(.) play video games(.) read(.) go rock climbing(.) go sailing(.) surf the net(.) travel(.)	→

144 Pragmatic Talk

TALKING ABOUT HOBBIES AS ACTIONS AND INCORPORATING FREQUENCY

during the fall / winter / spring / summer.
every chance I get.
every day / month / week / weekend.
on the weekends.
once a week / month / year.
whenever I get a chance.
whenever I have time.

Everyday Conversations 145

 # LESSON WRAP-UP

> **Remember**
>
> **to** use appropriate communication patterns when describing hobbies as nouns (or activities you enjoy) and as verbs. When using them as nouns, try to refrain from using any type of frequency at the end of the sentence as it will end up sounding awkward. But, you can place a frequency at the end of the sentence if describing the hobby as a verb.
>
> **that** you can use the adjective "main" to describe the hobby you do the most frequently. If you have several hobbies you can communicate those in conversation by using the conjunction "and."
>
> **that** hobbies like "rock climbing" and "mountain hiking" are gerunds, or words that are derived from verbs but by themselves are nouns. To transform these into verbs you must add "to go" before them.

 # SMALL TALK

Strange Hobbies: Extreme Ironing

Ironing is a fairly boring activity we do after we've washed and dried our clothes so that our duds look fresh, clean and unwrinkled. But, for some people , ironing has been made into an extreme sport and hobby. Basically, people that engage in this hobby iron clothes in an extreme way. They may iron clothes while sky-diving, on top of mountains, on the surface of frozen lakes, skiing, and water-water rafting.

lesson 13
My Favorite Things

 **INTRODUCTION**

TARGET TALK		
What's your favorite kind of **FAVORITE THING**?	➡	(I like) + **TYPE** + **FAVORITE THING**.
Why do you like **TYPE** + **FAVORITE THING**?	➡	(Because) it's / they're **REASON**.
What's your **TYPE** + **FAVORITE THING**?	➡	(My favorite **TYPE** + **FAVORITE THING** is) **NAME** or **TITLE**.
(Do you have) any other favorite kinds of **FAVORITE THING**?	➡	I like **TYPE** + **FAVORITE THING** as well.

✱ *Anything in (parentheses) is optional.*

BUILDING BLOCKS

EXPRESSIONS

QUESTIONS	STATEMENTS
What's your favorite kind of **FAVORITE THING**?	(I like) + **TYPE** + **FAVORITE THING**.
Why do you like **TYPE** + **FAVORITE THING**?	(Because) it's / they're **REASON**.
What's your **TYPE** + **FAVORITE THING**?	(My favorite **TYPE** + **FAVORITE THING** is) **NAME** or **TITLE**.
(Do you have) any other favorite kinds of **FAVORITE THING**?	I like **TYPE** + **FAVORITE THING** as well.

VOCABULARY

INFINITIVES / VERBS	TYPE	FAVORITE THINGS	REASON	OTHERS
to watch	action	movies	exciting	pop artist
to listen	romantic comedies	music	pleasant	
to eat	pop	food	delicious	
to read	hip-hop	book	interesting	
	Mexican			
	Korean			
	biographies			
	fiction			

 # LESSON REVIEW

A: What's your favorite kind of **FAVORITE THING**?

B: (I like) + **TYPE** + **FAVORITE THING**.

A: Why do you like **TYPE** + **FAVORITE THING**?

B: (Because) it's / they're **REASON**.

A: What's your **TYPE** + **FAVORITE THING**?

B: (My favorite **TYPE** + **FAVORITE THING** is) **NAME** or **TITLE**.

A: (Do you have) any other favorite kinds of **FAVORITE THING**?

B1: I like **TYPE** + **FAVORITE THING** as well.   B2: No, I only like **TYPE** + **FAVORITE THING**.

	GRAMMAR REFRESH
because	"because" is used to indicate "for the reason of". I like pop music because it's pleasant.
Countable and Uncountable Nouns	Movies and books are countable nouns and when referred to again, they'll typically take the plural pronoun "they" plus the plural form of "to be" "are" thus making "they're." I like biographies because they're interesting.
	*There are exceptions to be aware of with types of books. Biographies are countable, but "fiction" is uncountable. Therefore you'd use the pronoun "it" and the singular form of "to be" when mentioning fiction. I like fiction because it's interesting.
	Music and food are typically uncountable, so you'll want to use the pronoun "it" and the singular form of "to be" "is" when describing these. I like Korean food because it's delicious.
my	"my" is used to refer to something belonging to or associated with the speaker. My favorite movie is The Terminator.
as well	"as well" expresses in addition to. I like Mexican food. I like Korean food as well.
only	"only" expresses the meaning of "nothing more" than what was mentioned. I only like Mexican food.
EXTRA	"What?" is going to ask about something, while "Who?" is going ask about some person. When talking about a person's favorite music, you can ask them "What's your favorite kind of music?" which refers to the specific genre of music. We'll use "Who?" when asking for the name of the music artist.
	What is = What's ; They are = They're ; It is = It's ; Who is = Who's

Everyday Conversations

ROLE PLAY

DIALOGUE 1

A: What's your favorite kind of movie?
B: (I like) **action** (**movies**).
A: Why do you like action (movies)?
B: (Because) they're **exciting**!
A: What's your favorite **action movie**?
B: (My favorite action movie is) **The Terminator**.
A: (Do you have) any other favorite kinds of movies?

B1: Yes, I like **romantic comedies** as well.

B2: No, I only like **action movies**.

STRAIGHT TALK

A: What's your favorite kind of movie?
B: **I like action movies because they are exciting! I like romantic comedies as well**!

DIALOGUE 2

A: What's your favorite kind of music?
B: (I like) **pop** (**music**).
A: Why do you like pop (music)?
B: (Because) it's **pleasant**.
A: Who's your favorite **pop artist**?
B: (My favorite **pop artist** is) **Michael Jackson**.
A: (Do you have) any other favorite kinds of music?

B1: Yes, I like **hip-hop** as well.

B2: No, I only like **pop** (**music**).

STRAIGHT TALK

A: What's your favorite kind of music?
B: **I like pop music because it's pleasant. I like hip-hop as well**.

DIALOGUE 3

A: What's your favorite kind of food?
B: (I like) Mexican (food).
A: Why do you like Mexican (food)?
B: (Because) it's delicious.
A: What's your favorite Mexican food?
B: (My favorite Mexican food is) tacos.
A: (Do you have) any other favorite kinds of food?

B1: Yes, I like Korean (food) as well.   B2: No, I only like Mexican (food).

STRAIGHT TALK

A: What your favorite kind of food?
B: I like Mexican food because it's delicious. I like Korean food as well.

DIALOGUE 4

A: What's your favorite kind of book?
B: (I like) biographies.
A: Why do you like biographies?
B: (Because) they're interesting.
A: What's your favorite biography?
B: (My favorite biography is) Into the Wild.
A: (Do you have) any other favorite kinds of books?

B1: Yes, I like fiction as well.   B2: No, I only like biographies.

STRAIGHT TALK

A: What's your favorite kind of book?
B: I like biographies because they're interesting. I like fiction as well.

Everyday Conversations

PRACTICE

DO IT YOURSELF!

Write your two dialogues of your own!

DIALOGUE 1

A:
B:
A:
B:
A:
B:
A:
B:

DIALOGUE 2

A:
B:
A:
B:
A:
B:
A:
B:

 **LISTEN AND FILL IN**

A : What's your favorite kind of food?

B : _____.

A : Why do you like Korean food?

B : _____.

A : What's your favorite Korean food?

B : _____.

A : Do you have any other kinds of favorite food?

B : _____.

 **TALKING TIPS**

#1 "*What's your favorite kind of*~?" and "*What's your favorite*~?" are different in that "*What's your favorite kind of*~?" is asking for a general response, while "*What's your favorite*~?" is asking for a more detailed response. When a person asks you "*What's your favorite kind of food*?", they're asking you what type of food you like (Korean? Indian? Mexican?). If a person asks you "*What's your favorite food*?", it's more typical to narrow your answer down to a specific food item you like (tacos, pizza, club sandwich, etc.). When asking for general information on what music a person likes, you'll use "*What's your favorite kind of*~?" and asking for specific details, you'll ask "*Who's your favorite artist*?" View the table below for more examples.

Continued on next page ➡

What's your favorite kind of movie?	I like dramas.
What's your favorite movie?	My favorite movie is *Oldboy*.
What's your favorite kind of book?	I like fiction.
What's your favorite book?	My favorite book is *Catcher in the Rye*.
What's your favorite kind of music?	I like rock (music).
Who's your favorite rock (music) artist?	My favorite rock (music) artist is Aerosmith.
What's your favorite kind of food?	I like Indian (food).
What's your favorite food?	My favorite food is chicken curry.

#2 While this lesson has primarily focused on singular favorites, you can also use pluralize the conversation. View the able below for examples on pluralizing the conversation.

What are your favorite kinds of movies?	I like dramas and romantic comedies.
What are your favorite movies?	My favorite movies are *Oldboy* and *The Terminator*.
What are your favorite kinds of books?	I like fiction and autobiographies.
What are your favorite books?	My favorite books are *Catcher in the Rye* and *Into the Wild*.
What are your favorite kinds of music?	I like rock (music), pop (music) and hip-hop.
Who are your favorite music artists?	My favorite music artists are Aerosmith, Maroon 5 and Jay Z.
What are your favorite kinds of food?	I like Indian (food), Korean (food) and American (food).
What's your favorite food?	My favorite food is chicken curry, bibimbap and hamburgers.

#3 You also have the option to shorten your answer if you choose to do so. But be sure to be mindful of whether the favorite thing is a countable or uncountable noun. If you say "*I like action movies*", you're using "*action movies*" which is countable because of "*movies*." But, you can also say, "*I like action*." "*Action*" is a genre of movie, and therefore uncountable. You need to pay close attention to this especially when you're giving a reason as to why you like something to ensure you use the correct pronoun and be verb in your reason. View the table below for examples.

I like action movies (because they're exciting).	I like action (because it's exciting).
I like Mexican food (because it's delicious).	I like Mexican (because it's delicious).
I like pop music (because it's pleasant).	I like pop (because it's pleasant).
I like biographies (because they're interesting).	I like fiction (because it's interesting).

Pragmatic Talk

#4 Books, movies and music are going to have variances in their types. Some of the types or genres will regularly have an object (action movies) and others regularly do not (comedies).

For instance, we do not say "*I like biography books*", we say "*I like biographies.*"

For movie genres such as "*comedy*" and "*drama*", we say "*I like comedies / dramas*" and not "*I like comedy movies / drama movies.*"

For music, we usually do not put the word "*music*" after "*hip-hop*" or "*heavy metal.*"

What's your favorite kind of book?		autobiographies. biographies. fiction. non-fiction.
What's your favorite kind of movie?	I like / I enjoy	comedies. dramas. documentaries. romantic comedies. thrillers.
What's your favorite kind of music?		hip-hop. heavy metal.

When asking what a person's favorite book or movie title or music artist for the aforementioned types, follow the patterns in the table below.

	BOOKS		MOVIES		MUSIC
What's your favorite	autobiography? biography? fiction book*? non-fiction book*?	What's your favorite	comedy? drama? documentary? romantic comedy? thriller?	Who's your favorite	hip hop artist? heavy metal artist?

*when asking a question, it's normal to put the word "book" after "fiction" and "non-fiction."

COMMUNICATION VARIATIONS

QUESTION			
What's your favorite	kind of type of	→	book? food? movie? music?

POSSIBLE ANSWERS			
I like I enjoy	→	**MOVIES** action (movies). adventure (movies). animation (movies). comedies. documentaries. dramas. horror (movies). romantic movies. romantic comedies. thrillers.	**MUSIC** classical (music). country (music). Heavy metal. Hip-hop. K-pop. Pop (music). reggae music. rock (music).

QUESTION			
Do you have any other favorite	→	kinds of types of	→ books? food? movies? music?

Pragmatic Talk

POSSIBLE ANSWERS

FOOD

American (food).

Canadian (food).

Chinese (food).

French (food).

Indian (food).

Japanese (food).

Korean (food).

Mexican (food).

BOOKS

autobiographies.

biographies.

business books.

classic literature.

fiction.

non-fiction.

political books.

self-help books.

POSSIBLE ANSWERS

I also like ➡		
I also enjoy		
	type + favorite thing(s)(.)	
I like ➡		as well.
I enjoy		too.

 # LESSON WRAP-UP

> **Remember** →
>
> **the** difference between "What's your favorite kind of~?" and "What's your favorite~?" "What's your favorite kind of~?" will be asking for a type of something you consider your favorite, while "What's your favorite~?" requires an answer more specific such as a title or a name.
>
> **that** you can pluralize your questions and answers to provide a longer and more detailed response.
>
> **to** be mindful of how countable and uncountable nouns work especially when providing a reason for why you find "something" your favorite. Be sure to use the correct pronoun and "to be" verb.

 # SMALL TALK

My Faves

A common, but informal, way to say "My favorites" or "My favorite" is using "My faves" or "My fave." Someone may ask you, "What's your favorite kind of movie?" If you have several different kinds of movies you like, you can answer with, "My faves are action, comedies and horror" or "Action, comedies and horror are my faves." If it's only one specific kind of movie, then you can say "My fave is action" or "Action is my fave."

lesson 14
Making an Appointment with a Friend

INTRODUCTION

TARGET TALK	
Would you like to **PLAN** this / next week?	➡ Sure, I'd like that. I'm sorry, I'd like that but I'm busy this / next week.
When?	
How about (this) / next **DAY**?	➡ Sure, I'm free (this) / next **DAY**. I'm sorry, I can't make it (this) / next **DAY**.
What time would you like to meet?	
How does **TIME** sound?	➡ **TIME** sounds great!
How about **TIME** instead?	➡ I'm sorry, I've got something going on at **TIME** (this) / next **DAY**. I'll meet you at **MEETING PLACE** at **TIME** (this) / next **DAY**. Sounds great!

* Anything in (parentheses) is optional.

Everyday Conversations

 **BUILDING BLOCKS**

EXPRESSIONS	
QUESTIONS	**STATEMENTS**
Would you like to **PLAN** <u>this</u> / <u>next</u> week?	Sure, I'd like that. I'm sorry, I'd like that but I'm busy <u>this</u> / <u>next</u> week.
When?	
How about (<u>this</u>) / <u>next</u> **DAY**?	Sure, I'm free (<u>this</u>) / <u>next</u> **DAY**. I'm sorry, I can't make it (<u>this</u>) / <u>next</u> **DAY**.
What time would you like to meet?	
How does **TIME** sound?	**TIME** sounds great!
How about **TIME** instead?	I'm sorry. I've got something going on at **TIME** (<u>this</u>) / <u>next</u> **DAY**. I'll meet you at **MEETING PLACE** at **TIME** (<u>this</u>) / <u>next</u> **DAY**. Sounds great!

VOCABULARY			
PLAN	**DAY**	**TIME**	**EXPRESSIONS**
go hiking	Sunday	one	I can't make it.
have dinner	Monday	two	I've got something going on.
grab some drinks	Tuesday	three	Sounds great!
go shopping	Wednesday	four	Sure!
	Thursday	five	Ok
	Friday	six	**MEETING PLACE**
	Saturday	seven (o'clock)	mountain
		eight	restaurant
		nine	pub
		ten	mall
		eleven	**OTHERS**
		twelve	week
			free
			busy
			meet

 # LESSON REVIEW

A: Would you like to **PLAN** this / next week?

B1: Sure, I'd like that. When?   B2: (I'm) sorry. I'd like to, but I'm busy this / next week.

A: How about (this) / next **DAY**.

B1: Sure, I'm free (this) / next **DAY**. What time would you like to meet?   B2: No, I can't make it (this) / next **DAY**.

A: How about **TIME**?

B1: **TIME** sounds great!   B2: (I'm) sorry, I've got something going on at **TIME** (this) / next **DAY**. How about **TIME** instead?

A: Ok, I'll meet you at **MEETING PLACE** at **TIME** (this) / next **Day**.

	GRAMMAR REFRESH
this	Used to indicate a present period of time. *I'm busy this week.*
next	Used to indicate a period of time coming immediately after the present period of time. *I'm busy next week.*
that	"that" is being used in this lesson to refer to something previously mentioned. A: *Would you like to have dinner?* B: *Sure, I'd like that.*
at	"at" is used here to indicate a particular place (*at XYZ Mountain*) and to indicate time (*at one o' clock*).
but	"but" is used to introduce a point contrasting with one already mentioned. *I'd like to, but I'm busy.*
instead	Used to suggest an alternative or substitute to. A: *How about two o' clock?* B: *How about three o' clock instead?*
	I would = I'd ; I am = I'm ; cannot = can't; I will = I'll

# ROLE PLAY

DIALOGUE 1

A: Would you like to **go hiking** this week?

B1: Sure. I'd like that! When?

B2: (I'm) sorry. I'd like to, but I'm busy this week.

A: How about (this) **Thursday**?

B1: Sure, I'm free (this) **Thursday**. What time would you like to meet?

B2: (I'm) sorry, I can't make it (this) **Thursday**.

A: How about eleven (o' clock)?

B1: **Eleven (o' clock)** sounds great!

B2: (I'm) sorry, I've got something going on at **eleven (o' clock)** (this) **Thursday**. How about **twelve (o' clock)** instead?

A: Ok. I'll meet you at **ABC Mountain** at **eleven (o' clock)** this **Thursday**.
B: Sounds great!

STRAIGHT TALK

A: Would you like to go hiking this Thursday?
B: **Sure. I'd like that! What time would you like to meet**?

DIALOGUE 2

A: Would you like to **have dinner** this week?

B1: Sure. I'd like that! When?

B2: (I'm) sorry. I'd like to, but I'm busy this week.

A: How about (this) **Friday**?

B1: Sure, I'm free (this) **Friday**. What time would you like to meet?

B2: (I'm) sorry, I can't make it (this) **Friday**.

A: How does **five (o' clock)** sound?

B1: **Five (o' clock)** sounds great!

B2: (I'm) sorry, I've got something going on at **five (o' clock)** (this) **Friday**. How about **six (o' clock)** instead?

A: Ok. I'll meet you at **XYZ Restaurant** at **eleven (o' clock)** (this) **Thursday**.
B: Sounds great!

STRAIGHT TALK

A: Would you like to have dinner this week?
B: **Sure. I'd like that! What time would you like to meet**?

DIALOGUE 3

A: Would you like to **grab some drinks** next week?

B1: Sure. I'd like that! When?   B2: (I'm) sorry. I'd like to, but I'm busy next week.

A: How about next **Saturday**?

B1: Sure, I'm free next **Saturday**. What time would you like to meet?   B2: (I'm) sorry, I can't make it next **Saturday**.

A: How does **eight** (**o' clock**) sound?

B1: **Eight** (**o' clock**) sounds great!   B2: (I'm) sorry, I've got something going on at **eight** (**o' clock**) next **Friday**. How about **nine** (**o' clock**) instead?

A: Ok. I'll meet you at **ABC Pub** at **eight** (**o' clock**) next **Saturday**.
B: Sounds great!

STRAIGHT TALK

A: Would you like to grab some drinks next week?
B: **Sure. I'd like that! What time would you like to meet**?

DIALOGUE 4

A: Would you like to **go shopping** next week?

B1: Sure. I'd like that! When?   B2: (I'm) sorry. I'd like to, but I'm busy next week. all. Thank you.

A: How about next **Sunday**?

B1: Sure, I'm free next **Sunday**. What time would you like to meet?   B2: (I'm) sorry, I can't make it next **Sunday**.

A: How does **one** (**o' clock**) sound?

B1: **One** (**o' clock**) sounds great!   B2: (I'm) sorry, I've got something going on at **one** (**o' clock**) next **Sunday**. How about **two** (**o' clock**) instead?

A: Ok. I'll meet you at **XYZ Mall** at **eight** (**o' clock**) next **Saturday**.
B: Sounds great!

STRAIGHT TALK

A: Would you like to go shopping next week?
B: **Sure. I'd like that! What time would you like to meet**?

PRACTICE

DO IT YOURSELF!

Write your two dialogues of your own!

DIALOGUE 1

A:
B:
A:
B:
A:
B:
A:
B:

DIALOGUE 2

A:
B:
A:
B:
A:
B:
A:
B:

 **LISTEN AND FILL IN**

A : Would you like to have dinner this week?

B : _____ .

A : How about this Tuesday?

B : _____ .

A : How does two o' clock sound?

B : _____ .

A : Ok, I'll meet you at XYZ Restaurant at two o' clock this Tuesday.

B : _____ .

 **TALKING TIPS**

#1 If someone asks you for a potential appointment and you cannot commit to that appointment at the specific time your friend gives you, be sure to issue an apology first rather than just saying "*I can't make it*" or "*I've got something going on*." When refusing a person's offer or time suggestion it's common to issue the apology first then explain why you cannot commit to the appointment or time or day.

How about (this) Sunday?	I'm sorry, I can't make it this Sunday. I'm sorry, I've got something going on this Sunday. I'm sorry, I'm busy this Sunday.
How does one o'clock sound?	I'm sorry, I can't make it at one o' clock. I'm sorry, I've got something going on at one o' clock. I'm sorry, I'll be busy at one o' clock.

Continued on next page ➡

Everyday Conversations **165**

More, when someone asks you invites you to do something and you cannot make it, apologize, then say "*I'd like to*" to indicate that would like to have dinner with that person then use the conjunction "*but*" to introduce the contrasting point of "*I can't make it*." This makes your refusal sound politer.

Would you like to have dinner this week?	I'm sorry. I'd like to, but I'm busy this week.
	I'm sorry. I'd like to, but I can't make it this week.
	I'm sorry. I'd like to, but I have many things going on this week.
Would you like to have dinner this Sunday?	I'm sorry. I'd like to, but I'm busy this Sunday.
	I'm sorry. I'd like to, but I can't make it this Sunday.
	I'm sorry. I'd like to, but I've got something going on this Sunday.
Would you like to have lunch at five o' clock?	I'm sorry. I'd like to, but I'm busy at five o' clock.
	I'm sorry. I'd like to, but I can't make it at five o' clock.
	I'm sorry. I'd like to, but I have something going on at five o' clock.

#2 If you cannot meet at a specific time or day, you can use the word "*instead*" to present an alternative. If you cannot meet someone at two 'clock because you've got something going on, you can ask that person "*How about three* / *four* / *five etc. instead*?" This also applies to days of the week as well. If you cannot meet someone on Monday, you can ask them "*How about Tuesday* / *Wednesday* / *Thursday etc. instead*?"

How about Monday? How does Monday sound?	I'm sorry. I can't make it Monday. How about Tuesday instead?
How about one o' clock? How does one o' clock sound?	I'm sorry. I've got something going on at one o'clock. How about two o' clock instead?

#3 Typically, the person requesting an appointment with you already has a meeting place in mind. They'll normally end the conversation with a confirmation (Let's meet at *Place Name* at time <u>this</u> / <u>next</u> *Day*). If they do not establish a meeting place in their reconfirmation, you can ask "*Where would you like to meet*?" to gather information on a meeting place.

> A: Let's meet at one o' clock this Sunday!
> B: Where would you like to meet?
> A: Let's meet at ABC Department Store.

#4 Typically, appointments for future dates are made at the beginning of the hour (one o' clock). But, a person may also suggest 1:15 (one fifteen), 1:30 (one thirty) or 1:45 (one forty five). When stating these they may use they may actually use "*one fifteen*", "*one thirty*" or "*one forty five*" when establishing a time to meet. Or, they may also use a preposition of time. View the able below to see the three commonly used prepositions of time in conversation.

PREPOSITIONS OF TIME	
1: 15	one fifteen = a quarter past one.
1:30	one thirty = half past one.
1:45	one forty five = a quarter to two.

#5 You can also ask a person when they are free so you can make an appointment to meet up with that person.

ASKING FOR A FRIEND'S AVAILABILITY	
When are you free <u>this</u> / <u>next</u> week?	I'm free (<u>this</u>) / <u>next</u> **DAY**.
What time are you free <u>today</u> / <u>tomorrow</u>?	I'm free at **TIME**.
Are you free this week?	Yes, I'm free (<u>this</u>) / <u>next</u> **DAY**.
Are you free at **TIME**?	Yes, I'm free at **TIME**.

Everyday Conversations

COMMUNICATION VARIATIONS

MAKING AN APPOINTMENT WITH A FRIEND

Would you like to / Do you want to	**PLAN** go hiking(?) go shopping(?) have <u>breakfast</u> / <u>brunch</u> / <u>lunch</u>/ <u>dinner</u>(?) <u>grab</u> / <u>get</u> some drinks(?) get some coffee(?) go to the movies(?) play soccer(?) eat out(?) go to the park(?) visit Seoul(?)	this next	week? weekend? month?
		this on next	Monday? Tuesday? Wednesday? Thursday? Friday? Saturday? Sunday?
		this tomorrow	morning? afternoon? evening?

MAKING SUGGESTIONS FOR TIME | SHORT RESPONSES

How about *time*?
How does *time* sound?
Is *time* good?

→

AFFIRMATIVE
(*Time*) sounds <u>great</u> / <u>good</u>!
That'll be <u>fine</u> / <u>great</u> / <u>good</u>!

DECIDING A MEETING PLACE | SHORT RESPONSES

Where would you like to meet?
Where do you want to meet?

→

Let's meet at *Place Name*.
I can meet you at *Place Name*.
How about *Place Name*?

168 Pragmatic Talk

SHORT RESPONSES

AFFIRMATIVE

(Sure), I'd like that!

Sounds great / good!

Sounds like a plan!

NEGATIVE

Sorry, I'd like to, but I've got something going on.

Sorry, I'd like to, but I'm busy.

Sorry, I'd like to, but I'm busy this / next / on time indication.

ASKING ABOUT TIME

QUESTION	RESPONSE	
What time would you like to meet?	How about	time?
What time do you want to meet?	Let's meet at I'm free at I have time at	time.

SHORT RESPONSES

NEGATIVE

Sorry, I can't make it at time. Sorry, I'm busy at time.	(How about time instead?) (Can we meet at time instead?) (Let's meet at time instead.)

 # LESSON WRAP-UP

Remember

to be polite by apologizing when refusing a person's appointment request and day or time suggestion by prefacing your response with "(I'm) sorry."

also, when refusing someone's appointment to do something, preface your statement first with your apology then with "I'd like to" which indicates that you would like to do something with this person than use "but" to introduce your contrasting point.

to suggest alternative times and days using the word "instead" if you cannot make the specific time or day your friend has suggested.

to ask for a meeting place if the person has not given you one when they're reconfirming their appointment with you at the end of the conversation.

that although most people will plan an appointment at the beginning of the hour, they may also suggest a time that is a quarter past the hour, half past the hour or a quarter to the next hour.

 # SMALL TALK

Let's Hang Out

"Hang out" is an informal expression used to indicate getting together with a friend. There's usually no objective or plan to "hanging out", as it means to just spend time either by yourself or with another person. When a person says "Let's hang out this Friday" it means they want to spend time with you the Friday of that week. There may be no concrete plans, as "hanging out" could mean having dinner, getting drinks, getting coffee, going to the park or a number of other activities you do with friends.

SECTION 3

FREE TIME

> *"Courage doesn't happen when you have all the answers.
> It happens when you are ready to face the questions
> you have been avoiding your whole life."*
>
> **Shannon L. Alder**

lesson 15
Eating Out 1

 **INTRODUCTION**

TARGET TALK		
Are you ready to order?	→	(Yes, I'll have the) **MENU ITEM**, please. No, I need a little more time. Thank you.
How would you like that cooked? ** this question is for "steak" only*	→	(I'd like it (cooked)) medium rare.
Which side dish would you like?	→	(I'd like a / the) **SIDE DISH**.
(Would you like) any **TOPPING** on that?	→	Yes, thank you. No, on the side, please.
(Would you like) any appetizers?	→	Sure, the **APPETIZER** looks good. No, thank you. (That's all).
What would you like to drink?	→	(I'll have) (a) **BEVERAGE**, please.

* *Anything in (parentheses) is optional.*

Everyday Conversations

 # BUILDING BLOCKS

EXPRESSIONS

QUESTIONS	STATEMENTS
Are you ready to order?	(Yes, I'll have the) **MENU ITEM**, please.
	No, I need a little more time. Thank you.
How would you like that cooked? ** this question is for "steak" only*	(I'd like it (cooked)) medium rare.
Which side dish would you like?	(I'd like <u>a</u> / <u>the</u>) **SIDE DISH**.
(Would you like) any **TOPPING** on that?	Yes, thank you.
	No, on the side, please.
(Would you like) any appetizers?	Yes, the **APPETIZER** look(s) good.
	No, thank you. (That's all).
What would you like to drink?	(I'll have) (a) **BEVERAGE**, please.

VOCABULARY

MENU ITEM	SIDE DISH	TOP	APPETIZER	BEVERAGE	OTHERS
steak	(loaded) baked potato	parmesan cheese	chicken quesadillas	cola	medium rare
baked chicken	steamed broccoli	queso	mozzarella sticks	water	on the side
chicken cream				wine	appetizer
pasta			garlic bread rolls	beer	
chimichanga			onion blossom		

EXPRESSIONS

I need a little more time.

That's all.

LESSON REVIEW

A: Are you ready to order?

B1: (Yes, I'll have the) **MENU ITEM**, please.

B2: No, I need a little more time. Thank you.

FOR STEAK ONLY
A: How would you like that cooked?
B: (I'd like it (cooked)) medium-rare.

FOR STEAK AND BAKED CHICKEN
A: Which side dish would you like?
B: (I'd like <u>a</u> / <u>the</u>) **SIDE DISH**.

FOR CHICKEN CREAM PASTA AND A CHIMICHANGA
A: (Would you like) any **TOPPING** on that?

B1: Yes, thank you.
B2: No, on the side, please.

FOR APPETIZERS
A: (Would you like) any **APPETIZERS**?

B1: Sure, the **APPETIZER** look(s) good.
B2: No thank you. (That's all).

A: What would you like to drink?
B: (I'll have) (a) **BEVERAGE**. Thank you.

	GRAMMAR REFRESH
the	"*the*" is used here to indicate something that is assumed to be common knowledge. If you're in a restaurant where you know they serve steak, you'd tell your waiter "*I'll have the <u>steak</u>, please.*" "the" can also be used with non-countable nouns such as broccoli and baked chicken (*I'll have the <u>broccoli</u>.*) and plural countable nouns like "fries." (*I'll have the <u>fries</u>.*)
with	"*with*" is used to express accompaniment. *I'll have the steak with <u>a baked potato</u>.*
a / an	"*a*" and "*an*" typically precede indefinite, singular nouns. In this lesson they're used with the side dish, loaded baked potato. When ordering food, a person will use "the" before the main dish (steak) and use the indefinite article (a, an) before the side dish if the side dish is a single countable noun. *I'll have <u>the</u> steak / <u>baked chicken</u> with <u>a</u> loaded baked potato.* Indefinite articles like "*a*" can also come before some non-countable nouns like "*cola*" and "*beer.*" It's become more common to say "*I'd like a <u>cola</u> / <u>beer</u>*" as these tend to mainly be consumed from cans, bottles or glasses. But, it's not common to use an indefinite article before "*wine*" or "*water*", so keep this in mind when ordering a drink.
to	"*to*" marks the infinitive (base form of a verb) in this lesson. *to eat, to drink*
also	"*also*" marks an addition to. *I'll have the steak. I'll also have baked chicken.*
as	"*as*" is used here to describe the purpose an object holds. *I'd like the chicken quesadillas as <u>an appetizer</u>.*
that	"*that*" is used in this lesson to refer to something previously mentioned. A: *I'd like a <u>chimichanga</u>.* B: *Would you like queso on <u>that</u>?*
Subject Verb Agreement	Remember to conjugate the verb "to look" between countable nouns (quesadillas) and non-countable nouns (onion blossom). You'll need to add an "s" after non-countable nouns and nothing after a plural countable noun. *The <u>onion blossom</u> looks good. The <u>quesadillas</u> look good.*
	I will = I'll ; I would = I'd

Everyday Conversations 175

 # ROLE PLAY

DIALOGUE 1

A: Are you ready to order?

B1: Yes, I'll have the **steak**, please.   B2: No, I need a little more time. Thank you.

A: How would you like that cooked?
B: (I'd like it (cooked)) **medium-rare**.
A: Which side dish would you like?
B: (I'd like <u>the</u> / <u>a</u>) **baked potato**.
A: (Would you like) any appetizers?

B1: Sure, the **chicken quesadillas** look good.   B2: No, thank you. (That's all).

A: What would you like to drink?
B: (I'll have) (a) **cola**, please.

STRAIGHT TALK

A: Are you ready to order?
B: **Yes, I'll have the steak with a loaded baked potato and a cola to drink, please. I'd also like the chicken quesadillas as an appetizer**.

DIALOGUE 2

A: Are you ready to order?

B1: Yes, I'll have the **baked chicken**, please.   B2: No, I need a little more time. Thank you.

A: Which side dish would you like?
B: (I'd like the) **steamed broccoli**.
A: (Would you like) any appetizers?

B1: Sure, the **mozzarella sticks** look good.   B2: No, thank you. (That's all).

A: What would you like to drink?
B: (I'll have) **water**, please.

STRAIGHT TALK

A: Are you ready to order?
B: **Yes, I'll have the baked chicken with the steamed broccoli and water to drink, please. I'd also like the mozzarella sticks as an appetizer**.

DIALOGUE 3

A: Are you ready to order?

B1: Yes, I'll have the **chicken cream pasta**, please.

B2: No, I need a little more time. Thank you.

A: Would you like any parmesan cheese on that?

B1: Yes, thank you.

B2: No, on the side, please.

A: (Would you like) any appetizers?

B1: Sure, the **garlic bread rolls** look good.

B2: No, thank you. (That's all).

A: What would you like to drink?
B: (I'll have) **wine**, please.

STRAIGHT TALK

A: Are you ready to order?
B: **Yes, I'll have the chicken cream pasta with parmesan cheese and wine to drink. I'd also like the garlic bread rolls as an appetizer.**

DIALOGUE 4

A: Are you ready to order?

B1: Yes, I'll have **the chimichanga**, please.

B2: No, I need a little more time.

A: (Would you like) any queso on that?

B1: Yes, thank you.

B2: No, on the side, please.

A: (Would you like) any appetizers?

B1: Sure, the **onion blossom** looks good.

B2: No, thank you. (That's all).

A: What would you like to drink?
B: (I'll have) (a) **beer**, please.

STRAIGHT TALK

A: Are you ready to order?
B: **I'll have the chimichanga with queso on the side and a beer to drink. I'd also like the onion blossom as an appetizer.**

Everyday Conversations 177

PRACTICE

DO IT YOURSELF!

Write your two dialogues of your own!

DIALOGUE 1

A:
B:
A:
B:
A:
B:
A:
B:

DIALOGUE 2

A:
B:
A:
B:
A:
B:
A:
B:

 **LISTEN AND FILL IN**

A : Are you ready to order?

B : _____ .

A : Which side dish would you like?

B : _____ .

A : Would you like any appetizers?

B : _____ .

A : What would you like to drink?

B : _____ .

TALKING TIPS

#1 Sometimes a main menu dish will come with two sides. If this is the case, use the conjunction "*and*" to complete your statement.

TWO SIDE DISHES
A: Which two side dishes would you like? B: I'll have a baked potato and (the) steamed broccoli.

#2 Sometimes the first thing a waiter or waitress will ask you is if you want some appetizers. If this is the case they may ask you something along the lines of "*Would you like to start off with any appetizers*?" You can answer with either "*Yes, I'll have the~*" or "*Yes, I'd like the~*" and then provide the name of the appetizer you want and follow it up with the word "*please*." (*I'd like the chicken quesadillas, please*.)

If you do not want an appetizer, you can reply with a simple "*No, thank you*."

#3 The situation also comes up where you are not ready to order. If you are not ready, you can say "*I need a little more time*" or you can use one of the expressions in the table below.

NOT READY TO ORDER
A: Are you ready to order? B1: No, just a few more minutes, please. B2: No, sorry, not ready yet. B3: I need a bit / a tad more time, please.

COMMUNICATION VARIATIONS

ORDERING A MAIN DISH & APPETIZERS

QUESTION	RESPONSE VARIATIONS	
Are you ready to order? May I take your order?	I'll have the I'd like the I'll take the	**POSSIBLE MAIN MENU ITEMS** steak(.) baked / grilled / fried chicken(.) chicken cream / tomato / seafood / meatball pasta(.) grilled tilapia(.) fried shrimp(.) chimichanga(.) club sandwich(.)
Would you like any appetizers? Do you want any appetizers? Would you like to start with any appetizers?		**POSSIBLE APPETIZERS** chicken / beef / shrimp. mozzarella cheese sticks. garlic bread rolls. onion blossom. chili cheese fries. combo platter. chicken wings / tenders.
	Yes, the *appetizer*	look(s) good / great. sound(s) good / great.
	Yes, this / that *appetizer* *for non-countable items only! i.e. onion blossom	looks good / great. sounds good / great.
	Yes, these / those *appetizer* *for countable items only! i.e. chicken quesadillas	look good / great. sound good / great.

ORDERING A DRINK | TOPPINGS

I'll have I'll take I'd like	(a) cola. (a (bottle of)) beer. (a glass of) water. (a glass of) wine	Would you like Do you want	

EXTRA: STEAK PREFERENCE

I'd like it (cooked) I'll take it	rare. medium rare. well done.

* For appetizers, you can also say "I'd like the / I'll have the + appetizer.

with →

POSSIBLE SIDE DISHES

a / the baked potato, *please*.
(the) steamed broccoli / vegetables, *please*.
rice, *please*.
fries, *please*.
onion rings, *please*.
the soup of the day, *please*.
a salad, *please*.

NOTE: *When using "this" or "that" or "these" or "those" when ordering an appetizer, be sure to be pointing at the appetizer item on the menu!*

parmesan cheese
queso
cheese
sauce
dressing
jalapenos

→ on that?

AFFIRMATIVE RESPONSES

Yes, thank you.
Sounds good.

NEGATIVE RESPONSES

No, thank you.
No, on the side, please.

 # LESSON WRAP-UP

Remember →

that the article "a" can precede "cola" and "beer" but try not to use it with "wine" or "water" unless you referring to a counting unit
(a glass of wine / water ; a bottle of wine / water).

to use "please" at the end of your order to make your answer sound polite. Also, when refusing, be sure to say "thank you" at the beginning or end of your answer.

to use the conjunction "and" when you are offered more than one side dish (I'd like the baked chicken with a baked potato and steamed broccoli.)

that you may be asked if you want an appetizer either before or after your order.

when you are not ready to order to let your waiter or waitress know that are not ready using the expressions given in Talking Tips. Be sure to include "sorry" or "please" to express politeness.

 # SMALL TALK

Modern Toilet

Taiwan is home to several strangely themed restaurants and one of the strangest is "Modern Toilet". "Modern Toilet" is a bathroom themed restaurant where meals are served in miniature toilet bowls, drinks are served in miniature urinals and ice cream is served in miniature squat toilets. Keeping the tradition of the bathroom theme, you sit on toilet seats while you eat your food on a table resembling a kitchen sink with a glass top.

lesson 16
Eating Out 2:
Ordering Fast Food

 **INTRODUCTION**

TARGET TALK	
How may I take your order?	➡ (I'll take the) **FAST FOOD** combo, please. (No **CONDIMENT**).
(Would you like) French fries or onion rings (with that)?	➡ (I'll take the) French fries / onion rings.
(Would you like) barbecue sauce or honey mustard (with that)?	➡ (I'll take the) barbecue sauce / honey mustard.
(Would you like) mild or hot sauce (with that)?	➡ (I'll take the) mild sauce / hot sauce.
What would you like to drink?	➡ (I'll take) (a) **BEVERAGE**.
Would you like to upgrade your meal for fifty cents extra?	➡ Sure, thank you. No, thank you.
(How much do I owe you?)	➡ That'll be **PRICE**.

∗ Anything in (parentheses) is optional.

 **BUILDING BLOCKS**

EXPRESSIONS

QUESTIONS	STATEMENTS
How may I take your order?	(I'll take the) FAST FOOD combo, please. (No CONDIMENT).
(Would you like) French fries or onion rings (with that)?	(I'll take the) French fries / onion rings.
(Would you like) barbecue sauce or honey mustard (with that)?	(I'll take the) barbecue sauce / honey mustard.
(Would you like) barbecue sauce or honey mustard (with that)?	(I'll take the) mild sauce / hot sauce.
What would you like to drink?	(I'll take) (a) BEVERAGE.
Would you like to upgrade your meal for fifty cents extra?	Sure, thank you. No, thank you.
(How much do I owe you?)	That'll be PRICE.

VOCABULARY

FAST FOOD	SIDES	CONDIMENTS	PRICE	EXPRESSIONS	BEVERAGES
burger	French fries	mayo (mayonnaise)	four-fifty ($4.50)	Easy on the ice.	cola
cheeseburger	onion rings	ketchup	five-fifty($5.50)	Extra ice.	diet cola
chicken		barbecue sauce	six dollars ($6.00)	No ice.	lemonade
tender(s)		honey mustard	seven dollars ($7.00)		fruit punch
beef taco		mild sauce	fifty cents ($.50)		
		hot sauce			
		sour cream			

OTHERS
~upgrade your meal ; combo ; extra ; single / double

LESSON REVIEW

A: How may I take your order?
B: (I'll take the) **FAST FOOD** combo, please. (No **CONDIMENT**)
...
BURGER COMBOS
A: (Would you like) French fries or onion rings (with that)?
B: (I'll take (the)) <u>French fries</u> / <u>onion rings</u>.
CHICKEN TENDER COMBO
A: (Would you like) barbecue sauce or honey mustard (with that)?
B: (I'll take (the)) <u>barbecue sauce</u> / <u>honey mustard</u>.
BEEF TACO COMBO
A: (Would you like) mild or hot sauce (with that)?
B: (I'll take (the)) <u>mild sauce</u> / <u>hot sauce</u>.
...
A: What would you like to drink?
B: (I'll take) (a) **BEVERAGE**. (<u>Extra ice</u>. / <u>Easy on the ice</u>. / <u>No ice</u>.)
A: Would you like to upgrade your meal for an extra fifty cents?

B1: Sure, thank you. (How much do I owe you?)   B2: No, thank you. (How much do I owe you?)

A: That'll be **PRICE**.

	GRAMMAR REFRESH	
or	"or" is used to present two or more alternatives. *Would you like <u>French fries</u> or <u>onion rings</u>?*	
with	"with" is used to express accompaniment. *I'll take a single burger combo with <u>onion rings</u>.*	
that	"that" is used to refer to something previously mentioned. *I'll take the <u>single burger combo</u>. I take the onion rings with that.*	
the	"the" is used in this lesson to indicate an understood thing. "The" can be used with countable and uncountable nouns. *I'll take the <u>chicken tender combo</u> / <u>French fries</u>.*	
a	"a" is used in this lesson to mark a "single" item that beings with a consonant sound. It's optional to use it with the non-countable nouns in this lesson. *I'll take a <u>cola</u>.*	
for	"for" is used in this lesson to express how much money is to be paid. *Would you like to upgrade your meal for <u>fifty cents</u> extra?*	
and	"and" is used to join two or more words or phrases together into a complete statement. *I'll take a <u>single burger combo</u> and a <u>fruit punch</u>.*	
	I will = I'll	

Everyday Conversations

ROLE PLAY

DIALOGUE 1

A: How may I take your order?
B: (I'll take the) **single burger** combo, please. (No mayo).
A: (Would you like) French fries or onion rings (with that)?
B: (I'll take (the)) French fries.
A: What would you like to drink?
B: (I'll take) (a) **cola**. (Extra ice, please.)
A: Would you like to upgrade your meal for fifty cents extra?

B1: Sure, thank you.
(How much do I owe you?)

B2: No, thank you.
(How much do I owe you?)

A: That'll be **four-fifty**. ($4.50)

STRAIGHT TALK

A: How may I take your order?
B: **Single burger combo with French fries and a cola**, **please**. **No mayo**.

DIALOGUE 2

A: How may I take your order?
B: (I'll take the) **double cheeseburger combo**, please. (No ketchup.)
A: (Would you like) French fries or onion rings (with that)?
B: (I'll take (the)) **onion rings**.
A: What would you like to drink?
B: (I'll take) (a) **lemonade**. (Easy on the ice, please.)
A: Would you like to upgrade your meal for fifty cents extra?

B1: Sure, thank you.
(How much do I owe you?)

B2: No, thank you.
(How much do I owe you?)

A: That'll be **five-fifty**. ($5.50)

STRAIGHT TALK

A: How may I take your order?
B: **I'll take the double cheeseburger combo with onion rings and lemonade**, **please**. **No ketchup**.

DIALOGUE 3

A: How may I take your order?
B: (I'll take the) **chicken tender** combo, please.
A: (Would you like) barbecue sauce or
    honey mustard (with that)?
B: (I'll take (the)) barbecue sauce.
A: What would you like to drink?
B: (I'll take) (a) **diet cola**. (No ice, please.)
A: Would you like to upgrade your meal for fifty cents extra?

B1: Sure, thank you.   B2: No, thank you.
   (How much do I owe you?)   (How much do I owe you?)

A: That'll be **six dollars**. ($6.00)

STRAIGHT TALK

A: How may I take your order?
B: **Chicken tender combo with barbecue sauce and a diet cola**, **please**.

DIALOGUE 4

A: How may I take your order?
B: (I'll take the) **beef taco** combo, please. (No sour cream.)
A: (Would you like) mild or hot sauce (with that)?
B: (I'll take (the)) mild sauce.
A: What would you like to drink?
B: (I'll take) (a) **fruit punch**. (Extra ice, please.)
A: Would you like to upgrade your meal for fifty cents extra?

B1: Sure, thank you.   B2: No, thank you.
   (How much do I owe you?)   (How much do I owe you?)

A: That'll be **seven dollars**. ($7.00)

STRAIGHT TALK

A: How may I take your order?
B: **I'll take the beef taco combo with mild sauce and fruit punch**, **please**.
   No sour cream.

Everyday Conversations

 **PRACTICE**

DO IT YOURSELF!

Write your two dialogues of your own!

DIALOGUE 1

A:
B:
A:
B:
A:
B:
A:
B:

DIALOGUE 2

A:
B:
A:
B:
A:
B:
A:
B:

LISTEN AND FILL IN

A: How may I take your order?

B: _____.

A: Would you like French fries or onion rings with that?

B: _____.

A: What would you like to drink?

B: _____.

A: Would you like to upgrade your meal for fifty cents extra?

B: _____.

A: That'll be seven-fifty.

TALKING TIPS

#1 When you make a preference ordering a burger, make sure to use "*please*" after stating your preference if you didn't use it when you answered what you wanted for a meal. You can also use it in both your statements if you feel like being extra polite. Or if you want to get straight to the point, you can combine your burger combo with any condiment or topping you do not want (using "*without any*") on your burger using "*please*" at the end. View the table on the next page for further information.

Continued on next page ➡

PREFERENCE WHEN ORDERING A BURGER 1

Using "Please" Once
I'll take the single burger combo, please. No mustard.

Extra Politeness
I'll take the single burger combo, please. No mustard, please.

Straight to the Point
I'll take the single burger combo without any mustard, please.

You can also use the expression "*Hold the*~" and then state the condiment you do not want on your burger.

PREFERENCE WHEN ORDERING A BURGER: HOLD THE~
I'll take the single burger combo, please. Hold the mustard.

I'll take the single burger combo, please. Hold the mustard, please.

#2 You can also make preferences asking for more or less toppings or condiments on your burger. You can follow the pattern that we've used in this lesson for ice using "*Easy on the*" and "*Extra*." View the table below for these patterns.

MAKING SUBSTITUTIONS WHEN ORDERING A BURGER

Using "Please" Once
I'll take the single burger combo, please. Easy on the / Extra mustard.

Extra Politeness
I'll take the single burger combo, please. Easy on the / Extra mustard, please.

Straight to the Point
I'll take the single burger combo + with extra mustard / easy on the mustard, please.

#3 Upgrading a meal will come at a small extra price extra usually fifty cents to a dollar more. Other expressions for "*upgrading a meal*" will be "*upsize*" or "*super-size*." "*Extra*" may also be swapped out with the word "*more*."

UPGRADING A MEAL
Would you like to upgrade your meal for fifty cents extra / more?
Would you like to upsize your meal for fifty cents extra / more?
Would you like to supersize your meal for a dollar extra / more?

#4 There are a couple of different ways for someone to answer the question "*How much do I owe you?*" when ordering a meal from a fast restaurant. View the table below for these variations.

	HOW MUCH DO I OWE YOU?
$1.02	With single digit cents (1-9 cents) you will say the name of the letter "o" before providing the name of the single digit number. So, $10.08 would translate to "*ten O eight*." Using this pattern tends to be more common than saying how many dollars and how many cents. A / One + dollar / buck and two cents One + "O" two.*
$10.40	With double digit cents you can just say the name of the number. So, $12.67 would translate to "*twelve fifty-seven*". Using this pattern tends to be more common than saying how many dollars and how many cents. Ten + dollars / bucks and forty cents Ten + Forty*

You can also ask "*How much will that be*?" or "*How much*?" as different variations of "*How much do I owe you?*" "How much do I owe you?" adds a little personal touch to the question though.

#5 You do not always have to ask "*How much do I owe you*?" because once you've stated what your order is to the fast food clerk, they will probably automatically tell you what the price comes out to be.

COMMUNICATION VARIATIONS

ORDERING A COMBO

POSSIBLE FAST FOOD MENU COMBOS

(I'll take the)	(single) (double) (triple) →	(ham)burger →
(I'd like the) →		cheeseburger
(I want the)	chicken tenders beef / chicken taco hot dog foot long hot dog chili cheese dog fried chicken →	

MAKING SUBSTITUTIONS WHEN ORDERING A BURGER

No	**CONDIMENTS** ketchup(.) mayo(.)	
Hold the →	mustard(.) barbecue sauce(.) onions(.) special sauce(.)	(and)
Extra	lettuce(.) tomatoes(.)	
Easy on the	cheese(.) jalapenos(.) pickles(.)	

PAYING FOR YOUR ORDER AT A FAST FOOD RESTAURANT

QUESTIONS	RESPONSES			
How much do I owe you? How much will that be? → How much?	That'll be → That comes out to	one two three four five six seven eight nine ten →	dollar buck *informal*	→

	combo(.) set(.)	(with)	(French fries). (onion rings). (tater tots). (curly fries). (potato wedges). (chili cheese fries). (potato chips).

(CONDIMENTS)
(ketchup).
(mayo).
(mustard).
(barbecue sauce).
(onions).
(special sauce).
(lettuce).
(tomatoes).
(cheese).
(jalapenos).
(pickles).

and ➡	one two three four five six seven eight nine ten	eleven twelve thirteen fourteen fifteen sixteen seventeen eighteen nineteen twenty	➡	cent. cents. *see Talking Tips for more variations*

 # LESSON WRAP-UP

Remember

that there are different ways to make preferences when you're ordering a burger. If you want something taken off your burger just use "No" (or "Hold the~") then name the condiment or topping you do not want. If you want more of a condiment or topping, you can use the word "extra" before naming the condiment or topping and if you want a light amount of something say "easy on the~" then name your condiment or topping.

the different variations of how people will state a price. They may communicate a full response (five dollars and fifty cents) or they'll abbreviate it (five-fifty). Also remember that single digit cents will often be preceded by the name of the letter "o" ($3.06 = three O six).

that you do not have to ask "How much do I owe you?" to a fast food clerk as they'll automatically tell you the price of your order. Nonetheless, it's a decent expression to know when you need to know how much money you owe a certain person.

 # SMALL TALK

Heart Attack Grill

In "Sin City", Las Vegas, Nevada USA, there is a hamburger restaurant that goes by the name of "Heart Attack Grill". Founded by Jon Basso, the restaurant's menu boasts a single, double, triple, and quadruple "bypass" burger, flatliner fries deep fried in lard and pure sugar colas. The restaurant is decorated like a hospital with the waitresses dressed as scantily clad nurses who will "paddle" you if you do not finish all of your meal. As a bonus, if you weigh over 300 pounds (136 kg), you can get your meal for free.

lesson 17
Out for Drinks

 **INTRODUCTION**

TARGET TALK	
What can I get for you?	➡ I'd like~and~, please. (*answers will vary*)
(Would you like) anything else?	➡ Yes, I'll take~ as well. (*answers will vary*) No, (that's all). Thank you.
(Would you like to) start a tab or pay now?	➡ (I'd like to) <u>start a tab</u> / <u>pay now</u>.
(May I have your) name?	➡ **NAME**.

* *Anything in (parentheses) is optional.*

Everyday Conversations

 # BUILDING BLOCKS

EXPRESSIONS

QUESTIONS	STATEMENTS
What can I get for you?	I'd like~and~, please. (*answers will vary*)
(Would you like) anything else?	Yes, I'll take~ as well. (*answers will vary*) No, (that's all). Thank you.
(Would you like to) start a tab or pay now?	(I'd like to) start a tab / pay now.
(May I have your) name?	NAME.

VOCABULARY

MIXED DRINKS & COCKTAILS	COUNTING UNITS	LIQUOR	EXPRESSIONS	OTHERS
(a) Bloody Mary	(a) pitcher	soju	That's all.	beer
(a) rum and coke	(a) bottle	tequila		start a tab
(a) gin and tonic	(a) shot	whiskey		pay now
(a) White Russian	(a) double			
(a) Martini				

LESSON REVIEW

A: What can I get for you?
B: (I'd like)~and~, please. (*answers will vary*)
A: (Would you like) anything else?

B1: Yes, I'll take~ as well. (*answers will vary*)   B2: No, (that's all). Thank you.

A: (Would you like to) start a tab or pay now?
B: (I'd like to) start a tab / pay now.
A: (May I have your) name?
B: **NAME**.

	GRAMMAR REFRESH
a	"a" is an article used in this lesson to indicate a single item of something that begins with the sound of a consonant. *I'd like a pitcher of beer.*
of	"of" is placed after a quantifier this lesson and to express what will be contained within the stated quantifier. *I'd like a pitcher of beer.*
and	"and" is used to join two or more words or phrases together into a complete statement. *I'd like a pitcher of beer and a Bloody Mary.*
as well	"as well" expresses "in addition to." *I'd like a Bloody Mary. I'd like a White Russian as well.*
to	"to" marks an infinitive in this lesson. *I'd like to pay now.*
or	"or" is used to express two or more alternatives. *Would you like to start a tab or pay now?*
Singulars and Plurals	This lesson incorporates quantifiers (a pitcher, a bottle, etc). Whenever there is a single item, use "a" before the quantifier and leave it unmodified (*a pitcher of beer*). For anything that is more than "1", modify the counting unit by adding "s" at the end thus pluralizing it (*two pitchers of beer*).
	I would = I'd ; I will = I'll

Everyday Conversations

 # ROLE PLAY

DIALOGUE 1

A: What can I get for you?
B: (I'd like) a pitcher of beer and two Bloody Marys, please.
A: (Would you like) anything else?

B1: Yes, I'll take a shot of soju as well.   B2: No, (that's all). Thank you.

A: (Would you like to) start a tab or pay now?

B1: (I'd like to) start a tab.   B2: (I'd like to) pay now.

A: (May I have your) name?
B: Don.

STRAIGHT TALK

A: What can I get for you?
B: A pitcher of beer and two Bloody Marys, please. I'll take a shot of soju as well.

DIALOGUE 2

A: What can I get for you?
B: (I'd like) a shot of tequila and two shots of whiskey, please.
A: (Would you like) anything else?

B1: Yes, I'll take two bottles of beer as well.   B2: No, thank you. (That's all).

A: (Would you like to) start a tab or pay now?

B1: (I'd like to) start a tab.   B2: (I'd like to) pay now.

A: (May I have your) name?
B: Bob.

STRAIGHT TALK

A: What can I get for you?
B: I'd like a shot of tequila and two shots of whiskey, please. I'll take two bottles of beer as well.

DIALOGUE 3

A: What can I get for you?
B: (I'd like) a double whiskey and two rum and cokes, please.
A: (Would you like) anything else?

B1: Yes, I'll take a gin and tonic as well.   B2: No, (that's all). Thank you.

A: (Would you like to) start a tab or pay now?

B1: (I'd like to) start a tab.   B2: (I'd like to) pay now.

A: (May I have your) name?
B: Chucky.

STRAIGHT TALK

A: What can I get for you?
B: A double whiskey on the rocks and two rum and cokes, please. I'll take a gin and tonic as well.

DIALOGUE 4

A: What can I get for you?
B: (I'd like) a Martini and two White Russians, please.
A: (Would you like) anything else?

B1: Yes, I'll take a double whiskey as well.   B2: No, thank you. (That's all).

A: (Would you like to) start a tab or pay now?

B1: (I'd like to) start a tab.   B2: (I'd like to) pay now.

A: (May I have your) name?
B: Kandace.

STRAIGHT TALK

A: What can I get for you?
B: I'd like a Martini and two White Russians, please. I'll take a double whiskey as well.

PRACTICE

DO IT YOURSELF!

Write your two dialogues of your own!

DIALOGUE 1

A:
B:
A:
B:
A:
B:
A:
B:

DIALOGUE 2

A:
B:
A:
B:
A:
B:
A:
B:

 # LISTEN AND FILL IN

A: What can I get for you?

B: _____.

A: Would you like anything else?

B: _____.

A: Would you like to start a tab or pay now?

B: _____.

A: May I have your name?

B: _____.

TALKING TIPS

#1 You can also order beer from the tap. This beer is called interchangeably as "*on tap*" beer or "*draught beer*." If you'd like to know what's "*on tap*" or draught you can ask the bartender "*What do you have on tap*?" or "*What draught beers do you have*?" If you want to order an on tap / draught beer, you can tell your bartender "*I'd like a beer on tap, please*" or "*I'd like a draught beer, please*."

#2 There will be different variations when ordering liquor such as whiskey which were not covered in this lesson. Please view the table below for these variations!

	neat.	"*Neat*" means the whiskey is poured into a glass without ice and without being chilled or shaken.
I'd like a whiskey	on the rocks.	"*On the rocks*" means to add ice cubes to the liquor.
I want a whiskey	straight (up).	"*Straight (Up)*" means the whiskey or other liquor is shaken in a container, cooled with ice and then strained into a glass without the ice.
I'll take a whiskey		
I'll have a whiskey	with a twist.	"*With a twist*" means a lemon or lime will be added to your glass of liquor.
	with water.	"*With water*" means water will be added to the liquor to weaken the strong taste.

#3 Whenever you're ordering drinks for yourself or others, you can tell the bartender "*Put it on my tab*" if you've opened a tab. If using another's tab, tell the bartender "*Put it on Name's tab*." Be sure that you have permission to use *Name's* tab though!

Everyday Conversations

COMMUNICATION VARIATIONS

ORDERING DRINKS

QUESTION

What can I get for you?
common, casual

What would you like?
polite

What do you want?
direct

POSSIBLE ANSWERS

I'd like *polite*	a two three four five	bottle(s) glass(es) of mug(s) of pint(s) of pitcher(s) of
I want *direct*		shot of shots of single double singles of doubles of
I'll take *casual*		
I'll have *casual*		

COCKTAILS & MIXED DRINKS

Cosmopolitan(s).
cranberry and vodka(s).
Gin / Vodka and tonic(s).
Mojito(s).
rum / whiskey and coke(s).
Screwdriver(s).
Tequila Sunrise(s).
White / Black Russian(s).

beer.
*you can also use the name of the beer.

gin.
rum.
soju.
tequila.
vodka.
whiskey.
*you can also use the name of the liquor.

 # LESSON WRAP-UP

> **that** drinks, especially liquors and mixed drinks, will come with different variations and you can incorporate those variations into your dialogue!
>
> **Remember** → **that** beer and liquors will come with some type of quantifier. For beer, it's most often pitchers and bottles (I'd like <u>a pitcher of</u> / <u>a bottle of beer</u>). Liquors often come in "shots" (I'd like a shot of tequila). With most cocktails or mixed drinks, you do not have to state a quantifier. You'll just say "I'd like a ~" and then state the name of the cocktail or mixed drink.
>
> **to** drink responsibly!

 # SMALL TALK

Bottoms Up

The phrase "Bottoms Up!" will often be announced right before a person or a group of people drink a mug of beer. This expression has its origins in 16th Century England in which bar patrons would be duped by English Naval recruiters. The story goes that English Navy recruiters would buy a beer for a bar patron and then drop a shilling (a coin) into that individual's pewter tankard of beer. Upon discovering the shilling, the individual would be forced to join the Navy because he had been "paid" to do so.

As this practice became more common, clear glass bottoms were put on the pewter tankards so bar patrons could look underneath their pewter tankard (bringing the "bottom" up) to ensure no money was at the bottom. Thus, the expression "bottoms up" came into existence.

lesson 18
Plans for the Weekend

 **INTRODUCTION**

TARGET TALK	
What are your plans for the weekend?	➡ I plan on **WEEKEND PLAN** with my friends.
(Do you (all) have) any plans after that?	➡ We'll go to the **PLACE** (after **WEEKEND PLAN**). (That) sounds like **EXCLAMATION**!
(Would you) mind if I join you (all)?	➡ Not at all. You're more than welcome to join us!
(What's the) time and meeting place?	➡ We'll meet at **PLACE NAME** on Saturday around **PREPOSITION OF TIME**.

* *Anything in (parentheses) is optional.*

BUILDING BLOCKS

EXPRESSIONS

QUESTIONS	STATEMENTS
What are your plans for the weekend?	I plan on **WEEKEND PLAN** with my friends.
(Do you (all) have) any plans after that?	We'll go to the **PLACE** (after **WEEKEND PLAN**).
	(That) sounds like **EXCLAMATION**!
(Would you) mind if I join you (all)?	Not at all. You're more than welcome to join us!
(What's the) time and meeting place?	We'll meet at **PLACE NAME** on Saturday around **PREPOSITION OF TIME**.

VOCABULARY

WEEKEND PLAN	PLACE	EXPRESSIONS	OTHERS
bowling	museum	(Would you) mind if I join you (all)?	plans
singing karaoke	pub	Not at all.	weekend
having dinner	cinema	You're more than welcome to join us.	pub and grill.
shopping	café		department store

EXCLAMATIONS

That sounds like	fun!
	a blast!
	a great time!
	a fun time!

LESSON REVIEW

A: What are your plans for the weekend?
B: I plan on **WEEKEND PLAN** with my friends.
A: (Do you (all) have) any plans after that?
B: We'll go to the **PLACE** (after **WEEKEND PLAN**).
A: (That) sounds like **EXCLAMATION**! (Would you) mind if I join you (all)?
B: Not at all. You're more than welcome to join us!
A: (What's the) time and meeting place?
B: We'll meet at **PLACE NAME** on Saturday around **PREPOSITION OF TIME**.

	GRAMMAR REFRESH
with	Expresses accompaniment. *I'm bowling with my friends.*
my	Possessive pronoun which indicates something belonging to or associated with the speaker. *my friends*
after	Indicates the time following a period or event. *We'll go bowling after shopping.*
that	Refers to something previously mentioned. A: I plan on bowling. B: That sounds like fun!
to	Used to mark something or someone moving towards something. *We're going to the museum.*
the	Denotes an understood, definite noun. *the museum / cinema / café.* (each will be known to speaker and listener)
and	Used to join together two or more words or phrases. *I plan on bowling and going to the museum.*
at	Indicates a particular place, especially comes before the names of places. *I'm at ABC Department Store.*
on	Indicates a day of the week. *on Monday / Tuesday / Wednesday* etc.
around	means "approximately" *We'll meet around half past one.*
	We will = We will ; I am = I'm; What is = What's

Everyday Conversations

ROLE PLAY

DIALOGUE 1

A: What are your plans for the weekend?
B: I plan on **bowling** with my friends.
A: (Do you (all) have) any plans after that?
B: We'll go to the **museum** (after **bowling**).
A: (That) sounds like fun! (Would you) mind if I join you (all)?
B: Not at all! You're more than welcome to join us!
A: (What's the) time and meeting place?
B: We'll meet at **Mega Bowl** on Saturday around **noon**. (12:00 pm)

STRAIGHT TALK

A: What are your plans for the weekend?
B: **Bowling with my friends. After bowling**, **we'll go to a museum**. **You're more than welcome to join us**!

DIALOGUE 2

A: What are your plans for the weekend?
B: I plan on **singing karaoke** with my friends.
A: (Do you (all) have) any plans after that?
B: We'll go to the **pub** (after **singing karaoke**).
A: (That) sounds like a blast! (Would you) mind if I join you (all)?
B: Not at all! You're more than welcome to join us!
A: (What's the) time and meeting place?
B: We'll meet at **Superstar Karaoke** on Saturday around **half past five**. (5:30 pm)

STRAIGHT TALK

A: What are your plans for the weekend?
B: **I plan on singing karaoke with my friends**. **After that**, **we'll go to a pub**. **You're more than welcome to join us**!

DIALOGUE 3

A: What are your plans for the weekend?
B: I plan on **having dinner** with my friends.
A: (Do you (all) have) any plans after that?
B: We'll go to the **cinema** (after **having dinner**).
A: (That) sounds like a great time! (Would you) mind if I join you (all)?
B: Not at all! You're more than welcome to join us!
A: (What's the) time and meeting place?
B: We'll meet at **Jeff's Pub and Grill** on Saturday around **a quarter past six**. (6:15 pm)

STRAIGHT TALK

A: What are your plans for the weekend?
B: **Having dinner with my friends. After that, we'll go to the cinema. You're more than welcome to join us**!

DIALOGUE 4

A: What are your plans for the weekend?
B: I plan on **shopping** with my friends.
A: (Do you (all) have) any plans after that?
B: We'll go to the **café** (after **shopping**).
A: (That) sounds like a fun time! (Would you) mind if I join you (all)?
B: Not at all! You're more than welcome to join us!
A: (What's the) time and meeting place?
B: We'll meet at **ABC Department Store** on Saturday around **a quarter to two**. (1:45 pm)

STRAIGHT TALK

A: What are your plans for the weekend?
B: **I plan on shopping with my friends at ABC Department Store. After that, we'll go to a café. You're more than welcome to join us**.

Everyday Conversations 209

PRACTICE

DO IT YOURSELF!

Write your two dialogues of your own!

DIALOGUE 1

A:
B:
A:
B:
A:
B:
A:
B:

DIALOGUE 2

A:
B:
A:
B:
A:
B:
A:
B:

 **LISTEN AND FILL IN**

A : What are your plans for the weekend?

B : _____.

A : Do you have any plans after that?

B : _____.

A : Not at all! You're more than welcome to join us!

B : _____.

A : What's the time and meeting place?

B : _____.

 **TALKING TIPS**

#1 Asking someone "*Mind if I join you*?" is a casual and common way to ask the person's permission to join them for an event they'll be part of. Most people will answer this question with "*Not at all*" (meaning they do not mind, hence you're welcome to join that person) and follow it up with a "*You're more than welcome to join me / us*." If a person says, "*Yes, I do mind*" it means they do not want your company during the event. In this rare case, it's best to end the conversation right there as the event your friend has planned for the weekend may be exclusive to him or her and a small circle of friends or family. If you want to make "*Mind if you you*?" extra polite you can use "*Would you*" at the front of the statement.

#2 Using prepositions of time is another way for us to state a period of time. Remember that fifteen minutes past the hour is "*a quarter past*" the current hour, thirty minutes past the hour is "*half past*" the current hour and forty-five minutes past the hours is "*a quarter to*" the next hour. Others will also rely on the standard way to communicate time which is covered in the lesson "*Making an Appointment with a Friend*."

#3 You can use the question "*What are your plans for*~?" in a variety of different ways. View the table below for other ways to utilize this question.

What are your plans for	Christmas? vacation? your birthday?

COMMUNICATION VARIATIONS

WEEKEND PLANS

	for the →	weekend?
What are your plans (Do you have) any plans → What are you doing	this →	weekend? Friday? Saturday? Sunday?

ASKING PERMISSION TO JOIN YOUR FRIEND

(Would you) mind if I join you (all)?
more polite

(Do you) mind if I join you (all)?
more casual

Can I *more casual* **May I** *more polite* **(Would you) mind if I** *more polite* **(Do you) mind if I** *more polite*	→	tag along?

212 Pragmatic Talk

POSSIBLE RESPONSES

I plan on	→	bowling(.) cycling(.) having dinner(.) having drinks(.) having a picnic (.)		
I'm planning on I'm thinking about* *plans are not definite, but in consideration.	→	ice-skating(.) mountain hiking(.) shopping(.) skiing(.) singing karaoke(.)	with my	boyfriend. brother(s). co-workers. dad. friend(s). girlfriend. mom. parents. sister(s).
I plan on going to the I'm planning on going to the I'll go to the	→	amusement park(.) beach(.) cinema(.) club(.) movie theater(.) museum(.) park(.) pub(.) swimming pool(.)		

POSSIBLE RESPONSES

You're more than welcome to join <u>us</u> / <u>me</u>!
Sure! Come on out!
Sure! <u>I'd</u> / <u>We'd</u> love to have you!

 ## LESSON WRAP-UP

> Remember
>
> **that** you can use "Mind if I join you?" if you want to go along with a plan your friend has made with others. It's a casual, but polite way to ask a person's permission to join him or her. You can make it more polite by adding "Would you" at the front of the expression.
>
> **that** you can use different prepositions of time when establishing a time to meet your friend.
>
> **that** there are a variety of different ways to use the question "What are your plans for~?"

 ## SMALL TALK

Weekend Warrior

A "weekend warrior" is a term we use to describe a person who does a particular activity only on the weekend, typically involving drinking or partying. During the week-day they're a normal human being, but once work finished Friday evening they evolve into a weekend warrior!

lesson 19
Somewhere to Travel

 **INTRODUCTION**

TARGET TALK	
Where would you like to travel?	➡ (I'd like to travel to) **TRAVEL DESTINATION**.
Why **TRAVEL DESTINATION**?	➡ (I'd like) to see **TOURIST ATTRACTION**.
(Are there) any other places you'd like to visit?	➡ I'd also like to visit **TRAVEL DESTINATION** (to see **TOURIST ATTRACTION**). No, not really.
(Do you have) any plans to travel this year?	➡ Yes, I plan on travelling to **TRAVEL DESTINATION** this year. No, not this year. (Maybe next year.)

∗ Anything in (parentheses) is optional.

Everyday Conversations

 **BUILDING BLOCKS**

EXPRESSIONS

QUESTIONS	STATEMENTS
Where would you like to travel?	(I'd like to travel to) TRAVEL DESTINATION.
Why TRAVEL DESTINATION?	(I'd like) to see TOURIST ATTRACTION.
(Are there) any other places you'd like to visit?	I'd also like to visit TRAVEL DESTINATION (to see TOURIST ATTRACTION). No, not really.
(Do you have) any plans to travel this year?	Yes, I plan on travelling to TRAVEL DESTINATION this year. No, not this year. (Maybe next year.)

VOCABULARY

TRAVEL DESTINATION	TOURIST ATTRACTION	EXPRESSIONS	OTHERS
Paris	the Eiffel Tower	Not really.	to travel
China	the Great Wall	Not this year.	to see
New York	the Statue of Liberty	Maybe next year.	to visit
London	Big Ben		
Canada	Niagara Falls		
Dubai	Burj Khalifa		
Egypt	the Pyramids		
Rome	the Coliseum		

 # LESSON REVIEW

A: Where would you like to travel?
B: (I'd like to travel to) TRAVEL DESTINATION.
A: Why TRAVEL DESTINATION?
B: (I'd like) to see TOURIST ATTRACTION.
A: (Are there) any other places you'd like to visit?

B1: I'd also like to visit TRAVEL DESTINATION (to see TOURIST ATTRACTION).

B2: No, not really.

A: (Do you have) any plans to travel this year?

B1: Yes, I plan on travelling to TRAVEL DESTINATION this year.

B2: No, not this year. (Maybe next year.)

	GRAMMAR REFRESH
to	"to" serves two purposes in this lesson. The first function to mark an infinitive (*to travel*; *to visit*). The second function is indicate something or someone moving towards something or somewhere. (*I'm planning to travel to Paris.*)
the	"the" marks a definite or known noun. "The" will also commonly precede common nouns such as "statue", "tower", "coliseum" and "pyramid." But it will not precede "Big Ben", because there is no proper noun here; "big" is an adjective and "Ben" is a proper noun.
also	"also" is used to indicate "in addition to." *I'd like to travel to Paris. I'd also like to travel to Egypt.*
this	"this" is used here to indicate a period of time belonging to the present. *I'm planning to travel to Paris this year.*
and	"and" is used to join two or more words or phrases together make a complete statement. *I'm planning to travel to Paris and New York this year.*

Everyday Conversations

 **ROLE PLAY**

DIALOGUE 1

A: Where would you like to travel?
B: (I'd like to travel to) **Paris**.
A: Why **Paris**?
B: I'd like to see the **Eiffel Tower**.
A: (Are there) any other places you'd like to visit?

B1: I'd also like to visit **China** (to see **the Great Wall**).
B2: No, not really.

A: (Do you have) any plans to travel this year?

B1: Yes, I'm planning to travel to **Paris** this year.
B2: No, not this year. (Maybe next year.)

STRAIGHT TALK

A: Where would you like to travel?
B: **I'd like to travel to Paris to see the Eiffel Tower and also China to see the Great Wall**.

DIALOGUE 2

A: Where would you like to travel?
B: (I'd like to travel to) **New York**.
A: Why **New York**?
B: I'd like to see **the Statue of Liberty**.
A: (Are there) any other places you'd like to visit?

B1: I'd also like to visit **London** (to see **Big Ben**).
B2: No, not really.

A: (Do you have) any plans to travel this year?

B1: Yes, I'm planning to travel to **Paris** this year.
B2: No, not this year. (Maybe next year.)

STRAIGHT TALK

A: Where would you like to travel?
B: **I'd like to travel to New York to see the Statue of Liberty and also London to see Big Ben**.

DIALOGUE 3

A: Where would you like to travel?
B: (I'd like to travel to) Canada.
A: Why Canada?
B: I'd like to see Niagara Falls.
A: (Are there) any other places you'd like to visit?

B1: I'd also like to visit Dubai (to see Burj Khalifa).

B2: No, not really.

A: (Do you have) any plans to travel this year?

B1: Yes, I'm planning to travel to Canada this year.

B2: No, not this year. (Maybe next year.)

STRAIGHT TALK

A: Where would you like to travel?
B: **I'd like to travel to Canada to see Niagara Falls and also Dubai to see Burj Khalifa.**

DIALOGUE 4

A: Where would you like to travel?
B: (I'd like to travel to) Egypt.
A: Why Egypt?
B: I'd like to see the Pyramids.
A: (Are there) any other places you'd like to visit?

B1: I'd also like to visit Rome (to see the Coliseum).

B2: No, not really.

A: (Do you have) any plans to travel this year?

B1: Yes, I'm planning to travel to Egypt this year.

B2: No, not this year. (Maybe next year.)

STRAIGHT TALK

A: Where would you like to travel?
B: **I'd like to travel to Egypt to see the Pyramids and also Rome to see the Coliseum.**

Everyday Conversations

PRACTICE

DO IT YOURSELF!

Write your two dialogues of your own!

DIALOGUE 1

A:
B:
A:
B:
A:
B:
A:
B:

DIALOGUE 2

A:
B:
A:
B:
A:
B:
A:
B:

 **LISTEN AND FILL IN**

A : Where would you like to travel?

B : _____ .

A : Why New York?

B : _____ .

A : Are there any other places you'd like to visit?

B : _____ .

A : Do you have any plans to travel this year?

B : _____ .

TALKING TIPS

#1 There's different approaches you can take when answering a question like "*Where would you like to travel*?" You can answer with "*I'd like to travel to~*" or "*I'd like to visit~*" or you can also say "*I'd like to see~*" then state your travel destination.

Keep in mind if you use "*I'd like to see Travel Destination*" it generally describes that you want "*to see*" the general travel destination itself (*I'd like to see China*). Do not include a tourist attraction in this sentence as it will sound awkward (*I'd like to see China to see the Great Wall*).

Normally, when we use "*to see*", it's reserved for seeing famous tourist attractions. (*I'd like to see the Great Wall*.)

#2 Asking a person "*Do you have plans to travel this year*?" is a commonly asked question among friends and there are a variety of ways to state your answer. If you are feeling definite about travelling somewhere within the present year you can begin your answer with "*I plan on~*", "*I'm planning to~*", "*I'll probably~*" or "*I'm going to~*."

If there's some hesitance or uncertainty, you should begin your answer with "*I may~*" or "*I might~*".

If you're considering travelling somewhere for the year you should being your answer with "*I'm thinking about~*" or "*I'm considering~*."

#3 There are also different times to travel. Look at the table below and see the different periods of time you can use when answering a question that asks you if you have any plans to travel.

I'm planning to travel to **TRAVEL DESTINATION**	this next	fall month year
I plan on travelling to **TRAVEL DESTINATION**		
I'm going to go to **TRAVEL DESTINATION**	during	Christmas. my vacation. the summer
I'm going to visit **TRAVEL DESTINATION**		

Everyday Conversations

COMMUNICATION VARIATIONS

QUESTIONS	POSSIBLE RESPONSES
Where would you like to travel? Where do you want to travel?	I'd like to I want to
Are there any other places you'd like to visit? Are there any other places you want to visit?	I'd also like to I also want to I'd like to I want to
(Do you have) any plans to travel <u>this</u> / <u>next</u> year? Do you plan to travel <u>this</u> / <u>next</u> year?	I'm planning to *definite I'll probably *high possibility I may *possibility I might *possibility I'm going to *definite I plan on *definite I'm thinking about *considering I'm considering *considering

	go to travel to visit	*Travel Destination*(.)	to see	*Tourist Attraction.*
		Travel Destination, <u>too</u> / <u>as well</u>(.)		
	go to travel to visit	*Travel Destination*(.)	this year. next year.	
	going to travelling to visiting			

Everyday Conversations

 # LESSON WRAP-UP

> **Remember**
>
> **the** different approaches you can provide an answer to the question "Where would you like to travel?" You can substitute the word "travel" with "visit" or vice versa. You can also use "see", but understand that "see" is typically used for particular tourist attractions in the travel destination being visited.
>
> **that** you may be certain, uncertain or considering travelling somewhere else, so keep this mind when providing an answer if a person asks you "Do you have any plans to travel this year?"
>
> **that** there are different, more detailed time periods you can provide in an answer to the question "Do you have any plans to travel this year?"

 # SMALL TALK

My Way or the Highway

"My Way or the Highway" is an idiom said to express towards another that he or she can accept your way of doing things or they can leave. You'll usually hear this idiom spoken by a boss, a parent or other superior who wants you to conform to their "way of doing things" or you'll risk being excluded (kicked off onto the highway to fend for yourself).

lesson 20
At the Airport: Customs and Immigration

 **INTRODUCTION**

TARGET TALK		
		Welcome to **COUNTRY**.
May I see your passport and visa documentation?	➡	Yes, here you are.
Where are you coming from?	➡	((I'm) (coming) from) **COUNTRY**.
What's the purpose of your visit?	➡	(I'm here) **PURPOSE** (for # weeks / months / until the **ORDINAL NUMBER**).
Have you been to **COUNTRY** before?	➡	Yes, (this is my **ORDINAL NUMBER** time). No, (this is my first time).
(Do you have) anything to declare?	➡	Yes, **DECLARATION**. (No, I have) nothing (to declare).

✱ *Anything in (parentheses) is optional.*

Everyday Conversations

 # BUILDING BLOCKS

EXPRESSIONS

QUESTIONS	STATEMENTS
May I see your passport and visa documentation?	Yes, here you are.
Where are you coming from?	((I'm) (coming) from) **COUNTRY**.
What's the purpose of your visit?	(I'm here) **PURPOSE** (until the **ORDINAL NUMBER**).
Have you been to **COUNTRY** before?	Yes, (this is my **ORDINAL NUMBER** time). No, (this is my first time).
(Do you have) anything to declare?	Yes, **DECLARATION**. (No, I have) nothing (to declare).

VOCABULARY

COUNTRY	PURPOSE	DECLARATION	ORDINAL NUMBER	OTHERS
Korea	on business	nothing	first (1st)	passport
America	to visit family and friends	a bottle of wine	second (2nd)	visa documentation
Canada	for tourist purposes	a carton of cigarettes	third (3rd)	
France		a box of tea	fourth (4th)	
Australia		a package of tea	fifth (5th)	
China			tenth (10th)	
			fifteenth (15th)	
			twentieth (20th)	
			thirtieth (30th)	

EXPRESSIONS

Here you are.

 **LESSON REVIEW**

A: Welcome to **COUNTRY**.
   May I see your passport and visa documentation?
B: Yes, here you are.
A: Where are you coming from?
B: ((I'm) (coming) from) **COUNTRY**.
A: What's the purpose of your visit?
B: (I'm here) **PURPOSE** (until the **ORDINAL NUMBER**).
A: Have you been to **COUNTRY** before?

B1: Yes, (this is my **ORDINAL NUMBER** time).   B2: No, (this is my first time).

A: (Do you have) anything to declare?

B1: Yes, **DECLARATION**.   B2: (No, I have) nothing (to declare).

	GRAMMAR REFRESH
until	"until" means "up to the point of time mentioned." I'm here until the tenth.
the	"the" is used here to mark a period of time (date). I'm here until the tenth.
this	"this" is used in this lesson to refer to a period of time associated with the present. This is my first time.
my	"my" is used to refer to something belonging to associated with the speaker. This is my first time.
to	"to" is used to mark an infinitive. to visit, to declare, etc.
and	"and" is used to join together two or more words or phrases together in a statement. Here is my passport and visa documentation.
in	"in" is used in this lesson to describe being within an area. I'm here in America.
	I am = I'm ; What is = What's ; have not = haven't

Everyday Conversations

ROLE PLAY

DIALOGUE 1

A: Welcome to **Korea**. May I see your passport and visa documentation?
B: Yes, here you are.
A: Where are you coming from?
B: ((I'm) (coming) from) **America**.
A: What's the purpose of your visit?
B: (I'm here) **on business** (until the **fifteenth**).
A: Have you been to **Korea** before?

B1: Yes, (this is my **fifth** time).   B2: No, (this is my **first** time).

A: (Do you have) anything to declare?

B1: Yes, **a bottle of wine**.   B2: (No, I have) nothing (to declare).

STRAIGHT TALK

Here is my passport and visa documentation. I'm here in Korea on business until the fifteenth.

DIALOGUE 2

A: Welcome to **Canada**. May I see your passport and visa documentation?
B: Yes, here you are.
A: Where are you coming from?
B: ((I'm) (coming) from) **France**.
A: What's the purpose of your visit?
B: (I'm here) **for tourist purposes** (until the **twentieth**).
A: Have you been to **Canada** before?

B1: Yes, (this is my **second** time).   B2: No, (this is my **first** time).

A: (Do you have) anything to declare?

B1: Yes, **a carton of cigarettes**.   B2: (No, I have) nothing (to declare).

STRAIGHT TALK

Here is my passport and visa documentation. I'm here in Canada for tourist purposes until the twentieth.

DIALOGUE 3

A: Welcome to **Australia**. May I see your passport and visa documentation?
B: Yes, here you are.
A: Where are you coming from?
B: ((I'm) (coming) from) **America**.
A: What's the purpose of your visit?
B: (I'm here) **to visit family and friends** (until the **thirtieth**).
A: Have you been to **Australia** before?

B1: Yes, (this is my **third** time).   B2: No, (this is my **first** time).

A: (Do you have) anything to declare?

B1: Yes, **a box of tea**.   B2: (No, I have) nothing (to declare).

STRAIGHT TALK

> Here is my passport and visa documentation. I'm here in Australia to visit family and friends until the thirtieth.

DIALOGUE 4

A: Welcome to **America**. May I see your passport and visa documentation?
B: Yes, here you are.
A: Where are you coming from?
B: ((I'm (coming) from) **China**.
A: What's the purpose of your visit?
B: (I'm here) **on business** (until the **tenth**).
A: Have you been to **America** before?

B1: Yes, (this is my **fourth** time).   B2: No, (this is my **first** time).

A: (Do you have) anything to declare?

B1: Yes, **a package of coffee beans**.   B2: (No, I have) nothing (to declare).

STRAIGHT TALK

> Here is my passport and visa documentation. I'm here in America on business until the tenth.

PRACTICE

DO IT YOURSELF!

Write your two dialogues of your own!

DIALOGUE 1

A:
B:
A:
B:
A:
B:
A:
B:

DIALOGUE 2

A:
B:
A:
B:
A:
B:
A:
B:

 **LISTEN AND FILL IN**

A: Welcome to China. May I see your passport and visa documentation?

B: _____.

A: Where are you coming from?

B: _____.

A: What's the purpose of your visit?

B: _____.

A: Have you been to China before?

B: _____.

A: (Do you have) anything to declare?

B: _____.

 **TALKING TIPS**

#1 It's possible that other questions may be asked at through customs and immigration at the airport once you've reached your destination. View the table below for these extra questions and possible responses.

POSSIBLE QUESTIONS	POSSIBLE RESPONSES
How long will you be staying?	I'll be staying until the *ordinal number*. I'll be staying for # <u>days</u> / <u>weeks</u> / <u>months</u>.
Where will you be staying?	I'll be staying with my <u>family</u> / <u>friend</u>(s). I'll be staying at *ABC Hotel*. I'll be staying in *City*.
Are you carrying ten-thousand dollars of cash ($10,000) or more?	Yes, I am. No, I am not.
How many bags do you have?	I have # bag(s).

#2 Ordinal numbers are used to indicate the position of something in a list or rank. We use ordinal numbers in this lesson to express the date (I'll be here until the <u>tenth</u>) and to express the number of times one has been to a country (This is my <u>first</u> time).

#3 A declaration is a good or property of your which is subject to tax in your country of arrival. A customs and immigration official at the airport will always ask you if you have anything to declare. If you do not have anything, you can just reply with "nothing." But, if you have purchased something, especially a food or drink, you'll have to declare it.

Everyday Conversations

COMMUNICATION VARIATIONS

QUESTION	POSSIBLE RESPONSES
What's the purpose of your visit? ➡	I'm here ➡ for tourist purposes(.) on business(.) to visit friends and family(.)

POSSIBLE RESPONSES

| until the → | 1st first.
2nd second.
3rd third.
4th fourth.
5th fifth.
6th sixth.
7th seventh.
8th eighth.
9th ninth.
10th tenth.
11th eleventh.
12th twelfth.
13th thirteenth.
14th fourteenth.
15th fifteenth. | 16th sixteenth.
17th seventeenth.
18th eighteenth.
19th nineteenth.
20th twentieth.
21st twenty first.
22nd twenty second.
23rd twenty third.
24th twenty fourth.
25th twenty fifth.
26th twenty sixth.
27th twenty seventh.
28th twenty eighth.
29th twenty ninth.
30th thirtieth.
31st thirty first. |

| for → | <u>one</u> / <u>a</u>
<u>two</u> / <u>a couple of</u>
<u>three</u> / <u>a few</u>
four
five
six
seven
eight
tine
ten
eleven
twelve
thirteen
fourteen
fifteen
sixteen
seventeen
eighteen
nineteen
twenty | → | days.
months.
weeks. |

 # LESSON WRAP-UP

> **Remember**
>
> **that** there could be more questions directed towards you when you arrive at the airport customs and immigration area. The questions in this lesson are typically the most common, but be sure to study the extra questions listed in Talking Tips #1!
>
> **that** we use ordinal numbers to tell the date and to indicate the number of times we've been to the country of destination.

 # SMALL TALK

Different Ways to Say "Nothing"

When going through customs and immigration at an airport, you're often going to be asked the question by an official at the airport, "Do you have anything to declare?"

If you're a casual traveller, you'll probably have nothing to declare. With that being said, there are different ways to say "Nothing" which are commonly used by native speakers.

The first way is to say "Nada" which is Spanish for "Nothing."
 A: Do you have anything to declare?
 B: Nada.

Another way is to say "Zip" which is slang for "Nothing."
 A: Do you have anything to declare?
 B: Zip.

The last way is to say "Zilch" which is also slang for "Nothing."
 A: Do you have anything to declare?
 B: Zilch.

Pragmatic Talk
Everyday Conversations
실생활편

발행일	2017년 3월 24일 초판 인쇄
	2017년 3월 30일 초판 발행
저　자	하이랩 컨텐츠연구소
발행인	LEE AMY HEE K
발행처	하이랩 주식회사
등록번호	제2016-000159호
주　소	서울특별시 영등포구 양산로19길 8, 219호(당산동3가)
대표전화	02-704-2227
이메일	hilabcorp@daum.net

정가 14,800원

ISBN 979-11-960670-0-7 13740

이 책은 저작권법에 따라 보호받는 저작물이므로 무단전재와 복제를 금합니다.
잘못된 책은 구입하신 서점에서 교환해 드립니다.